First Edition

A DEAD CAT ON YOUR TABLE

A new guide to culture wars and how not to lose them

By Peter York

Illustrations by **Martin Rowson**

And contributions from *Byline Times* editors

BB

London, United Kingdom

This book is dedicated to Dennis Stevenson, my inspirational former business partner in a variety of enterprises. – Peter York

As ever, for Anna, Fred and Rose with all my love, and also for Paul Dacre, Rupert Murdoch and the rest of the gang for all the shits and giggles. – Martin Rowson

Byline Books
London, United Kingdom

First published in the United Kingdom of Great Britain and Northern Ireland by Byline Books, 2024

Text Copyright © Peter York, 2024

Illustrations Copyright © Martin Rowson, 2024

Cover design by Thomas Eagle

Production by Andrew Chapman, preparetopublish.com

Printed by DZS Grafik, Slovenia

ISBN: 978-1-9167541-2-6

Contents

There is one thing that is absolutely certain about throwing a dead cat on the dining room table – and I don't mean that people will be outraged, alarmed, disgusted. That is true, but irrelevant. The key point, says my Australian friend, is that everyone will shout, 'Jeez, mate, there's a dead cat on the table!' In other words, they will be talking about the dead cat – the thing you want them to talk about – and they will not be talking about the issue that has been causing you so much grief.

Boris Johnson on Sir Lynton Crosby's 'dead cat', from 'How Lynton Crosby (and a dead cat) won the election: "Labour were intellectually lazy", *Guardian*, 20 January 2016

At the next election we haven't got those three things, so we'll have to think of something else. It'll probably be a mix of culture wars and trans debate.

Lee Anderson, former Conservative MP for Ashfield, *Independent*, 14 February 2023

All I want is my country back. Now this may sound offensive to the liberal elite, but it's not offensive to my friends or family, my constituents and some of my donors.

Lee Anderson, Reform UK MP for Ashfield in his speech announcing his defection to Reform UK, 11 March 2024

"But the larger argument that I make is that politics is an artefact of culture. It's a reflection: Culture underwrites our politics."

Instead, 30 years later, Hunter sees America as having doubled down on the 'war' part – with the culture wars expanding from issues of religion and family culture to take over politics almost totally, creating a dangerous sense of winner-takes-all conflict over the future of the country.

James Davison Hunter, author of *Culture Wars: The Struggle to Define America* (1991), interviewed in *Politico* magazine, 2 May 2021

It was made pretty clear the plan is to run a culture war to distract from fundamental economic failings. It's not something I want any part of.

Iain Anderson, Cicero founder and former senior Conservative business leader, *Financial Times*, 13 February 2023

[Bannon] got it immediately. He believes in the whole Andrew Breitbart doctrine that politics is downstream from culture, so to change politics you need to change culture. And fashion trends are a useful proxy for that. Trump is like a pair of Uggs, or Crocs, basically. So how do you get from people thinking 'Ugh. Totally ugly' to the moment when everyone is wearing them? That was the inflection point he was looking for.

Carole Cadwalladr interview with Christopher Wylie about Cambridge Analytica, *Guardian*, 18 March 2018

To succeed, however, required some deception about the think tank's true aims. Fisher's partner in the venture, Oliver Smedley, wrote to Fisher saying that they needed to be 'cagey' and disguise their organisation as neutral and non-partisan. Choosing a suitably anodyne name, they founded the grandfather of libertarian think tanks in London, calling it the Institute of Economic Affairs. Smedley wrote that it was "imperative that we should give no indication in our literature that we are working to educate the public along certain lines which might be interpreted as having political bias. In other words, if we said openly that we were re-teaching the economics of the free market, it might enable our enemies to question the charitableness of our motives."

Jane Mayer, *Dark Money*, (2016), p. 80

Introduction

Things have been strange recently, haven't they? Particularly during and just after the Covid-19 pandemic. It was during the pandemic that my friend (let's call her Rachel) noticed her sister-in-law – a notable New Age veteran, soft leftie, keen on crystals, 'wellness', therapy of all kinds, with a side order of anti-business and anti Big Pharma especially – started behaving strangely. She was marching and shouting. She was visiting curious websites that told her that there was a plot to imprison the nation so that 'they' could take over. She believed that it was tied to vaccination and lockdowns and that it had all been planned for ages by a combination of Big Pharma and Big Money people. She also believed that George Soros and Bill Gates were involved, because she'd read it online somewhere. Bill Gates apparently wanted to put *minute* chips in the vaccine that would report on people's thoughts. She'd heard this from the local anti-vax group in a rather New Agey Devon town.

She also knew for sure – quoting a well-placed Australian friend – that they were hushing up the very high death rates from side effects of the Covid vaccination. Anthony Fauci, the American former chief medical advisor to the president of the United States, somebody she'd only recently heard (Fauci, not the Donald), was behind the hushing-up of the pandemic's Chinese origins. She'd heard from someone in her new marching and shouting milieu that he'd been very close to the Chinese.

She's convinced that 'mainstream media' like the BBC and ITN are lying to her, and they're all in on this. This makes family lunches very difficult indeed now that this woman is becoming obsessive, provoked by her 'secret knowledge'. She's taken against the *Guardian*, which she'd followed before, and she's started saying that Donald Trump was right after all.

And Rachel's got trouble even nearer home, *at* home in fact, where her son, who, like a fair few eighteen-year-old boys, has always lived mainly online, playing games that his parents don't get, had become even more isolated, practically never going out. The cheerful anarchy of his bedroom, cluttered with every kind of screen and keyboard, became and stayed weirdly tidy about a year ago. To her surprise Rachel decided she'd preferred it as it was.

He became starey eyed about one theme, namely that girls had it in for teenage boys like him. They had taken over. They took boys up and dropped them and he knew he would never have a girlfriend now. The one hero he'd admit to was a Canadian professor called Jordan Peterson whose book *12 Rules For Life: An Antidote to Chaos* had inspired the tidying. But there were others he visited on sites – new to her – called 4chan, and now 8kun, which she found very hard going and had to talk to her husband about. And there was Andrew Tate who, so her son had told her when he'd appeared on the old family TV, was being imprisoned in Romania on a trumped-up charge because he'd spoken up for men. Rachel wonders where she's gone wrong.

Why write this book now? There are several key reasons. For a start, it's a riveting subject, how the 'culture wars' came uninvited to Rachel's pleasant front door in middle-class west London. But the most important thing is that there's more where that came from. Culture warriors never give up. They want to take over the world and the new technologies that enable them to tell more plausible lies. As the world becomes ironically more autocratic as a result of 2024 elections happening on nearly every continent, your family and your friends will be subject to an unprecedented amount of culture wars propaganda, as will the rest of the world.

Culture wars stories will come both from the usual suspects we identify below but also from the great global cesspit of online comment and anecdote – often overlapping with the mainstream but 'embroidered' by anonymous editors with untraceable connections. And however tough and intellectually bulletproof you think you are, some of it will be surprising and disturbing.

When dramatic 'red button' stories – ones that work on our emotions and might change our feelings about the world and how we act – come our way out of the ether, we should have ways to understand them and track them to their sources, check them out and defend ourselves. Culture wars come naturally to the populists taking over everywhere, and, more generally, to all politicians who don't feel they can stand on their records alone. So they're shameless about making things up.

The theory and practice of post-war culture wars has been overwhelmingly developed in America. Our connections there are the strongest in the West; *we follow America* (remember Nigel Farage has been, for some years, Donald Trump's warm-up act!). American-style, US-trained culture warriors are now thoroughly embedded in the UK. At the time of writing, everyone says that the 2024 elections around the world will be the toughest and dirtiest ever. And dirty means culture war strategies designed to drive people mad with red button or 'wedge' issues. In the US November 2024 elections, Trump Republicans are *doing nothing but culture wars* because 'The Daily Hate' is at the heart of their kind of populism.

In the first part of this book, I'll explain my own 21st-century definition of culture wars. I'll look – briefly – at the 19th-century German and the 20th-century American definitions with their rather grandiose notions of a 'clash of values', as set out by, say, Republican Pat Buchanan in the 1990s and the American author of *Culture Wars* James Davison Hunter in 1991. All this before setting out my own view that, in the 21st century, culture wars are best described as a *political technology of storytelling employed by shameless people who want to win, whatever it takes.* A real 'clash of values' requires the opposing parties to have some values in the first place.

Culture warriors, like global marketeers, are *a profession with a set of techniques, not just a set of cultural convictions.* Well-paid people go to their desks in Westminster and Washington and work long days at it. They don't stand on soapboxes; they work with data. They don't coordinate real local volunteers; they dream up 'astroturf' (fake grassroots) organisations which do exactly what they're told. And now in 2024, and online rather than in person, the growing technology of deep-fakery makes the media part of the exercise both more lurid and provocative *and* more 'scientific' and predictable.

The science of identifying and targeting audiences online – a thousand times more micro-focused than the old world of mainstream media advertising strategies – means culture war pros can hit relevant influencers in tiny groupings with messages that seem surprisingly personal and resonant. And the rest of the world doesn't know it's happening.

There are *teams* of professionals at work here, people watching you and, with the help of the Silicon Valley empires, understanding you better than you do yourself. They can combine thousands of data points about your real interests, attitudes and behaviour. The famous Cambridge Analytica dossier in the *Observer* showed how collaboration with Facebook allowed CA to target people ever more relentlessly.

Then I'll set out the important background factors that shaped today's culture wars. The key ones are global collaboration with ideas (particularly with America), money and the ability it gives to hire or persuade people into your storytelling, and the importance of 'client media', national and international, legacy, new and social. People who run with the story, with no questions asked, are invaluable to culture warriors.

Next, I'll explain the areas in which culture wars operate – it's so *not* the economy stupid – and the sorts of people who prosecute them, the battle-hardened mercenaries. Then I'll tell some culture wars stories, about the people who've gone from being scholars, mainstream politicians or entertainers to being propagandists. The incidents – from unremarkable-seeming skirmishes through to pitched battles – show a story developing to the point where it becomes a 'wedge' issue – *where it divides us*. And I'll take you into situations where things really weren't as they seemed, and people weren't who they said they were.

In *Merchants of Doubt*, a book I read around 2010 – it was an American account of how 'public affairs' professionals worked to sow doubt about ideas like man-made climate change, or tobacco and health – the author describes going to a press launch organised by climate change sceptic lobbyists and takes in who's involved. He clocks the PRs, lobbyists, the 'sympathetic' journalists, the analysts and the various scientific expert witnesses, and realises that *the gang's all here.* He was seeing many of the same people and approaches he'd seen some years before when he was covering the tobacco and health story, and he'd watched what the tobacco lobby said and did, and who'd helped them.

At the end of 2020, when the pandemic was in full swing – lovely publishers' parties banned, bookshops closed, people totally distracted – Professor Patrick Barwise and I brought out our book *The War Against the BBC*, which described how 'hostile forces' were working to destroy our national broadcaster. It was evidence based, the result of two years of research (1,000 footnotes, 5 appendices, all that). We were surprised how our own ongoing assumptions were hugely changed by what we learnt. And by the line-up of people we learnt about who worked in parallel – I'm not saying it was always a planned, scheduled *conspiracy* – to do the Corporation down. People whose linkages – commercial *and* ideological – we simply hadn't recognised before. We weren't political geeks after all.

But since then, a lot of recent stories have seemed to feature these same people – by now our usual suspects – in action everywhere. Established commentators suddenly looked horribly predictable ("He would say that, wouldn't he?"). By then I could read the motives and the alliances. I knew the people and the organisations, the timeless tropes and the careerist moves. Front-page stories made sense when you knew where the journalists and their employers were coming from. Why that headline for, say, the story about the single rapist who'd 'gone trans' yet might go to a women's prison, made its own sense as a sort of *earworm*, one which might just worry clever friends, well-educated women. They were resonant somewhere well below people's rational defences.

I'm starting with 'stories', looking at the background of some high-profile people and events which show culture wars in action, following the motivations and the money and tracing some of the connections between the players (it's worth constantly emphasising that so many people, institutions and media platforms turn up again and again). In the second section, 'People and Places', I look more closely at some of the types who go to make up what I call the 'Metropolitan Illiberal Elite' and then, under 'Doors', look at some of the leading institutions that, in so many cases, lead the most proactive culture wars battles. Make no mistake, we aren't nearing the end of the fight against this. In fact, we aren't even nearing the end of the beginning. Best be armed and ready.

Part 1
Stories

1 What Exactly Is a Culture War?

I'm going to start with the official version. It's out of date, but it sets the stage for what actually happens now. There's a long history of culture war books and essays – overwhelmingly from America. The starting point for most of the academic writers is with the lovely German word *Kulturkampf* (these things demand a lovely German word). It translates as *cultural struggle* and describes the 19th-century struggle between the kingdom of Prussia – leader of a newly united Germany, with Bismarck as its leader (chancellor) – and the German wing of the Catholic Church. It all focused on who – church or state – should control education and the church hierarchy. It's been taken ever since to mean the struggles between belief systems – or 'values' – at various levels *within* a nation.

There's also a rhetorically important German moment in the development of the culture wars idea when a collection of European leftist intellectuals[1] were gathered in Frankfurt in 1923 and tried to think through – they were philosophers and sociologists after all – a new way of analysing and redirecting Europe and avoiding getting stuck in totalitarianism. This 'Frankfurt School' is just one factor in the background of the 'Euro-communism' of the 60s and 70s and it gave us several of the 60s counterculture's favourite philosophers, now largely forgotten. Still, they were interesting heroes for the kids who ran around doing the 1968 Paris 'events' and thought they were changing the world through street-fighting provocation.

But what *really* matters is that it gave a clutch of 21st-century

American right-wing culture war storytellers one of their absolutely favourite phrases – 'cultural Marxism' – which they regularly use to describe anyone a millimetre further left than, say, Joe Biden or Keir Starmer. People who they say are *subversive*. People who they couldn't credibly tag as *real* flat-out communists. People in the media, creative industries or academics. The 'left' is a very flexible idea in America because there really aren't many of them of any kind around. Their 'leftists' are at about the level of Andy Burnham, who sits only a few seats to the left of Starmer and nowhere that close to Jeremy Corbyn.

This dangerous conspiracy conveniently includes anyone who advances plans for change derived from anything the culture warriors don't like. Now you'll find people banging on about the Frankfurt School and cultural Marxists as an all-purpose catcall against universities, schools, cultural institutions and the media/creative industries. They seem to have got the stories in one hit with briefing papers from rightist American 'think tanks'. The culture warriors don't really know – and don't remotely care – about forgotten leftie philosophers. 'Cultural Marxism' is a favourite with American warriors because they're talking to a nation taught for a hundred years to have a knee-jerk reaction to even an utterance of the words 'Marxism', 'communism' or 'socialism'. Suella Braverman, who never heard an American right-wing cliché she didn't like, has used it constantly in her struggle to stay relevant.

The first crucial post-war American culture war – one that doesn't always feature as exactly that in the history books – was the 'Hollywood blacklist' of 1947—50.[2] It qualifies for me because the 'liberal elite' of New York and Hollywood was being framed and attacked for being unpatriotically left wing and dangerously influential. How dare they! It's a particularly performative bit of Cold War paranoia, but at the same time a training ground for later culture warriors. Its storytelling shaped Richard Nixon's rhetoric of the silent majority, the good decent 'ordinary American' and of course the McCarthy hearings of 1954. (One forgotten part of the McCarthy demonology then was the so-called Lavender Scare, the link that the McCarthyites made between communists, homosexuals and subversives.)

The McCarthy years gave us Roy Cohn, then a young lawyer on the prosecuting team, but, by the 1960s, a New York lawyer in private practice, favoured by mafia clients. *And mentor to Donald Trump.* Roy Cohn taught the young Donald Trump a great deal of what he applied in his business, celebrity and political life over the following 50 years. He taught Trump how to use lawyers to oppress his critics. He taught him how to lie big and double down relentlessly. He taught him how to play the man, not the argument, and he gave Trump his first training in how to be a demagogue – he was a promising pupil – and how to engage and distract shamelessly.[3]

Cohn is an interesting historical footnote, a predatory gay man despite these Lavender Scare prosecutions, a moral panic about homosexuals in the United States government which led to their mass dismissal from government service during the mid-20th century. He appears as a character in Tony Kushner's *Angels in America* and died of complications from AIDS in August 1986.[4] Trump had, of course, dropped him well before then.

The politician who brought cultural wars into Republican rhetoric in the 1990s was presidential hopeful Pat Buchanan, in his speech to the Republican National Convention of 17 August 1992:

> My friends, this election is about more than who gets what. It is about who we are. It is about what we believe, and what we stand for as Americans. There is a religious war going on in this country. It is a cultural war, as critical to the kind of nation we shall be as was the Cold War itself, for this war is for the soul of America. And in that struggle for the soul of America, Clinton and Gore are on the other side, and George Bush is on our side. And so, to the Buchanan Brigades out there, we have to come home and stand beside George Bush.[5]

A bit before that, in 1991, a thoughtful youngish academic, a professor of Sociology and Religious Studies at the University of Virginia called James Davison Hunter, published what became the definitive 20th-century book on the subject, *Culture Wars: The*

Struggle to Define America. In it he describes the historic context and the issues thrown up by the 60s, the cluster of rights movements starting with civil rights, women's rights – particularly abortion – and gay rights (though trans-specific rights didn't feature yet). It's thoughtful and considered but he's describing a different pre-internet world. He doesn't look at the almighty Heritage Foundation or the Cato Institute nor K Street (in Washington, the 'Madison Avenue' of lobbyists). There's nothing about the super-rich Koch Brothers (the inheritors of Koch Industries, America's second-largest private company), bankrolling the right-wing fightback. The book opens with an even-handed account of two San Francisco men who represent either side of the war. Chuck McIlhenny is a 43-year-old pastor of a small Presbyterian church not far from the Golden Gate Bridge roused to anger by Proposition S, proposed legislation which he believes is really designed to give legal recognition to homosexual unions. This, for McIlhenny, means "a fundamental attack upon Christianity, a fundamental attack upon the traditional biblical and marriage ideal".

The other side is Richmond Young, a gay man who lives in the same city but sees the potential legislation – it's subject to a referendum about which they're fighting – as "a movement toward greater equality and justice under the law".

Hunter's book did well enough in 1991, establishing the culture wars term, but Buchanan's speech the following year made him the TV and newspapers' favourite expert. This idea of a 'clash of values' between 'conservatives' and 'progressives', 'a struggle for the soul of America' is the Authorised Version, the idea of a continuing progressive attack on white picket fence America and the conservative backlash to it. It's between roughly equal forces, with that conservative backlash supposedly arising from the grass roots, of course.

But the great back-and-forth of political and social history isn't a complete explanation of 21st-century culture wars, so I believe – any more than Jon Ronson's marvellous BBC radio series, *Things Fell Apart*,[6] which tells great stories of US culture war incidents but doesn't explain the vested interests behind them. *You should follow the money. Dark Money* by the *New Yorker*'s Jane Mayer (2016) does precisely that. It shows how a group of right-wing billionaires, led by the Koch Brothers with huge investments in fossil fuel, and their plutocrat friends, spent billions over the years since the mid-70s developing a massively effective right-wing political propaganda machine *outside the political parties*. It was designed to protect the interests of people like themselves. *The ecology of the new professions and techniques that developed around this investment is the basis of the culture wars across the Western world now.*

One of the key architects of those Koch initiatives was an Englishman the brothers had met in America in 1977. Antony Fisher was an Etonian from a rich mine-owning family who built his first entrepreneurial fortune as a pioneer battery-chicken farmer at scale and co-founded the blandly academic-sounding Institute for Economic Affairs in London in 1955. It was the first – and most influential – right-wing 'advocacy' think tank in Westminster.

The IEA's founders Antony Fisher and Oliver Smedley, still working in Henry Fairlie's old Establishment London world, were concerned to be subtle rather than shameless. The nature of their deception was central to the 'brand values' of most right-wing London think tanks for the next 60 years; they gave an impression of an Oxbridge offshoot and their cluster of outsider scholars were dignified by titles like 'Fellow'. Antony Fisher had consulted the great right-wing fightback political philosopher Friedrich Hayek, then teaching at the LSE, about what he should do to prevent communism taking over the West. Hayek had told him to start "a scholarly institute" that would wage a "battle of ideas". If this worked, according to Hayek, he could change the course of history. In Jane Myer's crucial *Dark Money*, she describes the thinking behind the IEA's seminal approach:

> To succeed, however, required some deception about the think tank's true aims. Fisher's partner in the venture, Oliver Smedley, wrote to Fisher saying that they needed to be "cagey" and disguise their organisation as neutral and non-partisan. Choosing a suitably

anodyne name, they founded the grandfather of libertarian think tanks in London, calling it the Institute of Economic Affairs. Smedley wrote that it was "imperative that we should give no indication in our literature that we are working to educate the public along certain lines which might be interpreted as having political bias. In other words, if we said openly that we were re-teaching the economics of the free market, it might enable our enemies to question the charitableness of our motives.[7]

To give you some idea of how important the IEA has been at every level, you just have to know that *Liz Truss was one of theirs.* The IEA broke cover in 2022 and proudly claimed Truss for their own when she became PM and outed themselves as the power behind the throne.[8] Unwisely as it turned out. Fisher had done more than just inspire the Kochs and their friends – they included a Mellon banking heir among a nucleus of around 500 conservative super-rich donors – to fund the US right-wing think-tank/pressure group world like the Cato Institute, the Heritage Foundation and 'Americans for Prosperity'. Not surprisingly they're *particularly* keen on climate change-sceptical organisations and politicians – and particularly hostile to what they now call "eco-zealots" like Extinction Rebellion.

But Fisher didn't stop at that. In 1981 he also founded the completely spooky-sounding global Atlas Network, which helps the rapidly growing ecology of right-wing libertarian think tanks to set up around the world. They provide training, networking and money to the member organisations – 500 of them in more than 100 countries, which is impressive. Apart from a central concern with climate change, Atlas and its partners have been constantly identified by critics as being supportive of and funded by the tobacco industry. It would be fascinating to hear their conferences.

Fisher's granddaughter, Rachel Whetstone, is a serial global public affairs director for Silicon Valley companies like Google, Uber, Facebook and, currently, Netflix. She's married to Steve Hilton, David Cameron's former PR guru, the one with the shorts and the bike who taught the Camerons to be ostentatiously green. He's now a sometime

Fox News host – and a keen Donald Trump admirer (always follow the links).

This discursive tour round Antony Fisher, his family and his international linkages is important to show exactly what you have to do when you're faced with a culture wars pseudo-issue – a big distracting story which gets everybody worked up. *You have to follow the money.* You have to ask 'Who's paying for this?' and 'Who benefits from this?' then follow the connections. You couldn't find a more central figure than Fisher and every one of his connections – and there are many more, across the world – tells a story.

There *is* an 'ideological' component to the right-wing international lobby, but there's also simply an enormous amount of money at stake in culture wars – money in fossil fuels and regulation and potential tax cuts, all the things that concern the super rich. Although the lobby has engaged the US Christian right in the fight with its familiar attacks on abortion, LGBTQ+ and trans-specific groups, critical race theory and other alleged anti-Christian/anti-family teaching in schools and universities, it's worth remembering that the US religious ecology is very different from our own.

Like the American media ecology, US religion is a fragmented and divided 'free market'. It's a positively entrepreneurial sector. You can make good money running a 'church' in America (as you can running any radically partisan radio or TV station since Reagan scrapped the impartiality regulation the 'Fairness Doctrine' in 1987). They're not like us.

Despite these huge differences it's vital to understand the American precedents. They're not just influential, they're directly connected to us. In 2019 Matt d'Ancona – editor of the *Spectator* from 2006 to 2009, so one can assume hardly a raging leftie – wrote a crucial essay 'Bannon's Britain' on the news website Tortoise Media.[9] It explained the new world of UK politics, behind the traditional flummery of Parliament. It was about the unacknowledged power of Steve Bannon, Donald Trump's key strategist from 2016 to 2018, in our political world. He was very close to Boris Johnson, the Brexit rightists' favourite for PM at the time. Indeed, in the *Observer*, Carole

Cadwalladr had quoted Bannon talking in an American documentary about helping Johnson write his resignation speech as foreign secretary in Theresa May's government in July 2018 (meaning, in turn, his application to the Tory right to make him PM!).[10]

Bannon, who has that look of an angry divorced man who sleeps in his car, was the key architect of the early Trump strategy and the key link man with US groups to the right of the Trump administration. And key link man with the European far right, from Marine Le Pen to Viktor Orbán. He also defined his version of the culture wars grand strategy as "flood the zone with shit", i.e. don't just enrage and divide people but leave them confused and disoriented and looking for a strong leader.[11] An autocrat.

Johnson, according to d'Ancona, *hates* being connected to Bannon in media, and always denies it. He's got enough British social savvy to know that Bannon would never go down well with a majority of Brits – of any party. Johnson famously claimed, falsely, to be a 'one-nation' Tory – he'd lived in Islington for decades and there *is* a strong high-minded liberal strand on his mother's side. His grandfather was president of the European Commission for Human Rights (ECHR) from 1972 to 1982 (it's a crucial Tory *Daily Hate* target). In fact the 'one-nation' Tories who Johnson threw out of the party when he was prime minister came to loathe him (check out what Sir Max Hastings, Dominic Grieve, Damian Green, Anna Soubry and Rory Stewart say about Johnson).

America is central to our 21st-century culture wars in the UK. It's not just as an example – they developed so many of the approaches, the issues and so much of the rhetoric long before us – but in terms of hands-on advice and money. Liz Truss, the former British prime minister, recently spoke at the Republican Conservative Political Action Conference in Maryland, parroting a succession of Anglosphere far-right clichés and blaming British Establishment leftism (at communistical places like the Bank of England) for her fall. She then appeared on a panel with Steve Bannon and said that Conservatives in the UK and US "need a bigger bazooka in order to be able to deliver".[12] (She also appeared to endorse Steve Bannon's praise of the British far-right street-fighting man 'Tommy Robinson' in a follow-up session at CPAC.)[13] Truss is constantly in America, where she must see herself reflected flatteringly as a heroine and martyr whereas she's an embarrassment to the Conservatives back here and has *terrible* poll ratings.[14] What does she get from this world of power brokers and big money raisers, and what do they see in her? As d'Ancona explains in his Tortoise piece,[15] there are a lot of British quote merchants on this extraordinary circuit.

British politicians were right to worry about the Russian money that poured into Conservative Westminster as revealed by the 'Russia' report in 2020,[16] at least until the Ukraine invasion. But there's a fair bit coming from America. Influential UK-based right-wing think tanks like the IEA or the Henry Jackson Society often have US fundraising arms. Nobody's quantified it all yet but it's worth asking why rightist Americans – so often isolationists on other issues – support these Westminster warriors. Why was the curious online magazine *Spiked* worthy of the Kochs' money,[17] or for that matter, why did Tommy Robinson – a great hero of Steve Bannon's – get so much support from rich Americans?

The other crucial part of the UK culture wars' vertically integrated story is the constant support of the British national press. It's arguably the most unrepresentative in Europe; the Media Reform Coalition analyses show that somewhere between 85 and 90% of print sales are to reliably Conservative titles.[18] As the party moves to the right, like the Republicans, so do most of the papers. The BBC – far from being left wing – lives in terror of government and its hold on its finances and uses the watchword of 'impartiality' to avoid addressing culture wars issues too proactively or giving too many government spokespeople a really hard time.

The fact is that culture wars, as waged by our US Big Brothers and taught to UK right-wingers, are a suite of professional strategies used to win power and money. They're enacted by highly rewarded international mercenaries who develop a new emotive horror story every day and work it through with their favourite media platforms.

This process of modern culture wars looks entirely familiar to any group of London insider professionals who've worked in the extremely London-centric worlds of high-end marketing/PR/public affairs and lobbying. If you've got a story to sell but you want to avoid being seen as its author you look for 'third-party endorsements'. Credible-sounding people, organisations and media who'll say it for you.

Working like that – developing a major Culture Wars Story – needs a ton of money, the ability to return favours, with access to important people or prospects/job promotion, a lot of professional help from digital researchers and even private detectives, and a lot of 'client media', especially major newspapers, who'll take your stories/reports largely on trust.

One vital key 'third-party endorsement' sector for anonymous interests and donors is the group of opaquely funded right-leaning culture wars 'free-market' Westminster think tanks – including Policy Exchange – that Fisher inspired. Lobbyists call them 'wonk whores', meaning support them with donations and they'll support you. The kind of negotiation involved is described amusingly in the *Guardian*'s report of a Greenpeace sting on the IEA in 2015.[19]

Your case will return dressed in smart-sounding arguments delivered in reports by smart-sounding presenters with rather academic-sounding job titles. They will go and make it on your behalf to government and to influential media. Increasingly they take it wider now, not just to supportive mainstream media, starting with the national press, trusted never to question those reports' thinking or their funding. They go to broadcasters too, with their star presenters appearing across the range from ITV to GB News and Talk TV. They're also online now with Westminster panel discussions filmed for YouTube. And these polite and plausible people turn up with surprising regularity on the BBC, which, shamefully, given its commitment to 'impartiality' and its British mission to explain, has never helped viewers and listeners to understand who these people really are; it might as well take advertising revenue.

The other way of creating usefully distanced third-party endorsements of your arguments is through 'astroturfing'. It's a marvellous American name for any kind of ostensibly 'grassroots' organisation that's apparently come together to express the concerns of real people in real places but has actually been organised, scripted and 'cast' (staffed) by clever people in smart offices in Westminster. I remember, an age ago, Matthew Freud, the PR tycoon – son of Liberal MP Sir Clement, nephew of Lucian and then married to the TV entrepreneur Elizabeth Murdoch, daughter of Rupert (always follow the connections!) – telling me about his great-uncle, Vienna-born Edward Bernays, Sigmund Freud's nephew, and widely described as 'the father of public relations'. He's also seen as the father of astroturfing. Bernays' business invented a clutch of front organisations over the years of the 'Mothers for X' or 'Concerned citizens of Y town for Z initiative' kind (fill in an incontrovertibly vague high-minded-sounding mission). Bernays worked, by all accounts, with the CIA and the controversial US United Fruit Company in South America, which was often accused of interfering in politics where it operated.

Astroturf front organisations are a bit subtler now, taking greater pains to recruit token real people to their false fronts. And their work has been transformed by the internet, meaning the availability of bots and 'deepfakes' as well as the rapid development of AI. An early recruit to the potential of the astroturf idea was Dominic Cummings, the strategist credited with winning the referendum for Leave in 2016 and the 2019 election for the Conservatives. Cummings watched political technology developments in the US – and Russia, where he spent three years – long before British lobbying had got beyond the 'brown envelope' era. (giving MPs a wad of notes to ask questions in Parliament back in the 80s).[20]

In 2004, Cummings was running a small right-leaning think tank, the New Frontiers Foundation, with his friend James Frayne – husband of Rachel Wolf, daughter of the great *Financial Times* economics commentator Martin Wolf. Rachel Wolf was a co-author of the 2019 Conservative manifesto and co-founder with her husband, Frayne, of Public First, a research and PR company (always follow the connections!). Cummings wrote a strategy in 2004 to help the Tories destroy the BBC (he described it as 'the mortal enemy' of the Conservative Party). This included a clutch of the latest K Street Washington lobbyists' techniques, ranging from setting up a Fox News-type broadcaster in the UK (taken up later by GB News and Murdoch's Talk TV) along with instituting a group of BBC critics/scrutineers that sounds very much like astroturf and recruiting a 'fifth column' of BBC insiders who would provide embarrassing leaks and criticism.[21]

This strategy, apparently found via the Wayback Machine,[22] was characteristic of a new kind of Culture War objective – the destruction of a major British institution – and a new set of methods. Cummings was outlining the way forward for the New Westminster highly professional younger people who took over behind those nice tourist-friendly 18th-century elevations, developing an approach that had its finest hour in the Leave campaign.

The New Grifters

Becoming a culture warrior can really pay if you're a writer/ broadcaster/influencer. There always seem to be a variety of talent spotters looking for communicators with the right political talents. The first is the ability to attract and engage an audience, and the likely ability to attract a bigger one across more platforms with some better support behind you. The second is to have demonstrated your willingness – even enthusiasm – to write/ say the kind of thing your new sponsors like to see written. This could mean signs of a 'journey' towards their causes and their world view. Or just extraordinary flexibility in the face of money.

A bit of career realism shows that the people who have the big platforms and have the big money remain – even in the 2020s – extraordinarily dominant. Take our UK national press. People are forever arguing that its influence is declining fast as newspaper print sales fall and a variety of new platforms challenge them at every turn. That it's all becoming fragmented and democratised. That's not completely right but it does remind us of the formerly extraordinary sales, political unanimity and power of the pre-internet national press. Then as now, somewhere between 80% and 90% of print sales went to mainly Conservative-supporting newspapers with massive circulations.

Things may have changed in print sales terms, but the newspapers' content and their big names appear constantly on broadcasting, public speaking and online platforms. The 'names' often have associated broadcasting jobs like Talk TV – (now retreating online in the face of heavy losses), or the very right-leaning GB News. And 'mainstream' broadcasters – meaning 'public service' ones with Ofcom-regulated content – often take their themes and their guests from the big newspaper agenda.

And the point is that the jobs that matter, the best-rewarded ones by far, are *the names*, the presenters, the 'are you thinking what she's thinking' types, rather than geeky specialist section editors. Early this century a naughty friend told me about the rewards a mid-market tabloid was giving its big-name writers – the ones who did culture wars on a weekly basis. Back then – 20 years ago – the biggest man – it was a man then – was getting £850,000 a year, huge in 2004 terms. It descended through the ranks of the moderately famous to an irritating writer – someone who hadn't much to say, but you always knew what it would be – who was managing back then on just £450,000 a year. Nobody on the *Guardian* ever got that kind of money.

The Dutch historian Rutger Bregman, in an interview for Fox News (one they never ran) with their star presenter (later sacked) Tucker Carlson, said that Carlson was "a millionaire funded by billionaires". Carlson was, according to Jack Holmes in *Esquire*,[23] "tasked – along with the other talking heads of Fox News – with protecting the political and economic structure of the status quo while distracting the audience with propaganda that demonises immigrants as criminals". At the time of his sacking Mr Carlson was reported to be earning $20 million per annum.[24]

This helps explain why Boris Johnson, writing a column a week for the *Daily Telegraph*, back in 2009 said that his £250,000 pa was "chicken feed".[25] Every significant example seems to bear out the idea that a move to the right – but more than that, the culture wars right, as we're not talking about the small print of economic policy – means a much higher profile and a much better reward. People who follow in the path of Lord Beaverbrook, who'd said in the 1930s that he ran his newspapers "purely for the purpose of making propaganda and with no other object",[26] are very keen to find the talent they want in the most unlikely places. They like recanting 'formers' – former leftists, former communists even, former druggies and house-trained 'homos' who've seen the million-watt light from the tallest platforms. They like minority group members who can attack other minority members so it doesn't look too obviously 'ist'.

Every journalist for hire knows this. They know that if they fall out with their minority 'progressive' employers (there aren't many) the big people will welcome them, providing they'll start by writing something that says "as someone who believed in the progressive movement, I've been shocked by what I've seen on the left recently", followed by a long rant about, say, 'trans-activists' or the 'eco-zealots' and crazy anti-colonialists who want to destroy our history. "This is what I saw and heard." This kind of article is a staple of newspaper life. They've been commissioning versions of it for decades. If you can rise above your previous convictions, become less squeamish about the writing itself, let alone the headline the editors put on it, then you can pay the mortgage and afford some private education. And you may, somewhere along the way, start to enjoy it. You learn how to demolish hopeless young 'wokists' on a TV panel or to absolutely skewer them with cruel fun. You get big bonus points for right-wing fun, as Boris Johnson and Rod Liddle know. Right-wing fun can be disarming. You can say the unthinkable if it's wrapped in a sort of deadpan 'did he really say that?' way. "Give that man a £100,000 bonus!"

Although not essential, contacts always help. Back in the day, in happier times, being a gossip column partygoer reporter was an interesting start in life for an aspiring writer (and being a grown-up gossip column editor would put your children through school). I started to notice that some people I knew who were gossip column occasionals in the new world of toffs (by the later 80s they had to be *interesting* rich toffs, not just leftovers, and *important* plutocrats i.e. high profile money and *real* celebrities, no D-listers please) were sometimes being asked if they could identify their subjects' politics as well as go to their parties.

This is how it worked: the people who did the heavy lifting in newspapers, the political front pages and follow-ups would ask their connected young social friends whether they knew *anyone* – they all knew what was meant by anyone – who was going to any current leftie protest like the poll tax riots or any such 80s street protest-y thing. And could they point them out or give them a bit of background? And then there'd be, say, a front page 'second lead' continued on pages 2 and 3 that said young Lady This or That, daughter of an undeniably important toff, had been there in the crowd of protestors, wearing dungarees and looking very different from this earlier picture of her in a big taffeta Diana Spencer-type dress at a Big Party. Page 2 would explain that she'd gone to university and put it down to her hippie-activist boyfriend. All this was designed to show you how completely hypocritical these protest supporters were, *how out of touch.*

There's a new vocabulary for this sort of thing which derives from the old one – remember that nodding chorus in the 80s *Spitting Image* programmes shouting "political correctness gone mad!"?[27] But it's all been ramped up in a number of ways for the 21st-century culture wars. PC has become 'woke' – which is not only an all-purpose global catcall ('the woke mob') but which also, according to SMET (*Sun, Mail, Express, Telegraph*) *now completely runs the world.* According to the newspaper stories, top woke people don't just self-censor, they censor everyone else about everything. Apparently they shut them up and they 'cancel' them, getting them disinvited from speaking here or there, turning up outside venues in disorderly woke mobs and if all else fails, getting them sacked. The reality is altogether less intimidating.

This kind of coverage is meant to tell readers that whichever protest group the editors dislike is entirely composed of people so privileged – with money, contacts, fancy knowledge ('cultural capital') – that they can do absolutely anything they like – especially holding 'luxury beliefs'. This brilliant little tag – like 'virtue signalling' (invented by James Bartholomew in the *Spectator* in 2015) is meant as an unmistakable description of a new type of person, *someone whose political opinions are performative, invented to show their social/intellectual status.* They do it to show off. It's a development of a long-standing case against reformers – the motives of progressive 'do-gooders' were called into doubt in the Northcliffe papers over a hundred years ago – but now they're updated to take on new issues and global concerns. According to SMET these insincere perfor-mative people are nonetheless legion and extremely powerful; powerful enough to sway Cabinet ministers and change the law. So who exactly are they?

Who really runs the show is a crucial question in culture wars. If you can convince people that the people you hate *actually run the world now* and, at the same time, redirect any scrutiny away from the people who really do run the world, then you can name your price.

Political commentators are forever attempting to sell us easy memorable ideas about who really has the power and the money and can dictate what happens in this country. They're always on about shadowy 'elites', but they seem to have different elites to sell at different times. The one thing about people with an elite rap is that they're always insistent that *they* don't belong to that gang – the one they're encouraging you to hate, or indeed to any other elite groupings. This makes for some very odd accusations (like, for instance, Rishi Sunak or Jacob Rees-Mogg accusing anyone else on earth of being elite).

It was easier and more obvious when there was a more visible aristocracy and plutocracy and around them there was a whole political and administrative class. They were people who didn't all have stupendous money and power, but tended to come from pretty definable class/educational and occupational backgrounds. Since Henry Fairlie's crucial *Spectator* essay of September 1955 on 'The Establishment', that word stood in usefully for the elite enemy for convinced leftists well into the late 20th century. People still use the word all the time.

The response to the multiple revolutions of the late 60s on the emerging 'backlash right' from the later 70s on was to say all that had changed – or to suggest that those lucky people were much more deserving and public spirited than you realised. And that they were very good at running things – businesses and ministries. Back then the Establishment idea appealed to the residual British sense of class deference and at the same time, an emerging 'aspirational' feeling that an updated pastiche of the old upper-class life was desirable and buyable with lovely new 80s money – houses done up with massive curtains, stencilled walls and British mahogany furniture, Sloaney outfits, the lot.

These changes of mood meant that culture warriors could gaslight the world by saying the Rad Progs have actually become the Establishment who run the world. But now it's less clear who runs the show at all. So much of everything has been globalised and 'outsourced' over the last 40 years. The ownership of famous British companies, for example, isn't what you think. Boots is American owned. Quaker-founded Clarks Shoes of Somerset (1825) belongs to Viva Goods of Hong Kong, Rolls-Royce is owned by BMW – and so much production for 'British' companies is done in the Far East. And new people have come in – from the New Right – saying there's a new gang who run everything now.

According to this story, the new people apparently took over because they were hugely persuasive 'entrists' *with a political agenda they wanted to impose on everyone.* The current word for this sinister plot is 'woke'. The woke in this magical thinking have taken over the world, so the story goes, in order to make more ULEZ areas in British cities, to make sure that every last Brit gets diversity training, takes the knee every day and night and lives in daily fear of being cancelled if they say the wrong thing. You might ask how, if those really were the new masters of the universe's objectives, they got so far and took over absolutely everything. How did they get the qualifications and the corporate and organisational promotion if they did nothing but bang on about decolonising Britain's institutions? The very talkative Matthew Goodwin, Professor of Politics at Kent University, has been on every right-wing platform – and many 'centrist' ones as well – explaining his big idea about the New Elites who've taken over (there's more about Professor Goodwin and his supporters in Chapter 11). It strikes me – and even some of his academic peers – as preposterous borderline tosh. *But the newspapers like it,* and they buy it in pageloads. It's central to culture wars everywhere to have an 'elite' to hate.

For an example of how this particular rhetoric works, look at the TV channel GB News, launched in 2021 – which tells its viewers constantly that it's there for the real people, the decent people outside the Westminster bubble. (Seeing GB's presenter Jacob Rees-Mogg, Conservative MP for North East Somerset, an Etonian financier whose net worth is generally reckoned to be around £100 million and who has a large and delicious old house in Westminster as well as his constituency home, actually saying all this demotic stuff is quite marvellous to watch.)

Tracking culture wars means knowing who owns things. So who owns GB News? It's mainly two super-rich hedge-funders: Sir Paul Marshall, public school and Oxford, co-founder of Marshall Wace has 41.22% of voting shares. The Dubai-based Legatum Group, headed up by New Zealand-born Christopher Chandler – credited by *Fortune* magazine as a brilliant investor in distressed situations like 90s post-Soviet Russia – also has 41.22%.[28] The remaining voting shareholding is split between Lord (Michael) Farmer, supporter of Turning Point UK, and Angelos Frangopoulis, the GB station boss and an Australian journalist formerly at the Murdoch-owned Sky News Australia.

Chandler is the co-founder of the Legatum Institute, a conservative London think tank which, as I write, employs Zewditu Gebreyohanes, the former leading light of Restore Trust (see Chapter 5), as a senior researcher (always follow the connections). A third original investor in GB News was the US media giant Discovery, which had a 25% stake, sold for £8 million in 2022. Doesn't that all look like the traditional international right-wing plutocratic media story, rather than anything particularly grass roots? One of GB News's co-founders, Andrew Cole, was fiercely critical of the BBC to his LinkedIn followers in August 2020: the BBC was "possibly the most biased propaganda machine in the world", he told them.[29]

The BBC, however, actually belongs to us – i.e. to the 24.3 million licence fee payers; not to government, nor to City-owned commercial interests. It at least tries to be 'impartial' with varying results. The story about who has the money and the power may be more difficult to see now, but that doesn't mean, for instance, that the fourth Viscount Rothermere doesn't still own the *Daily Mail* and related businesses. It doesn't mean that Rupert Murdoch's News Corporation doesn't still own the *Sun* and the *Sunday Times*. It doesn't mean that inequality in the UK hasn't increased significantly in the last 40 years or that the 7% of privately educated children don't do significantly better in life than the rest. The mob of wildly woke radical progressives that's supposed to have taken over *everything* in the country is allegedly concentrated in academia, media, and institutions generally. The culture wars straw castle builders usually leave out the seriously super-rich and the globally powerful when they're bigging up this collection of bogeymen. That's because they're so often their paymasters, the institutions who help fund them in Washington and Westminster and the platform owners who publish or broadcast their engaging ideas. Everyone involved knows what the score is.

If you've been around in Westminster or Washington for years you'll know the names and the institutions. And you'll know from experience and all your research that most people out there *don't* know them. Especially in America where the gaslighting from Fox News and conspiracy theories generally has produced the Trump-loving MAGA majority in the Republican Party, which still believes The Donald won the 2020 election. It's a radical polarisation of the USA which might just provoke the next civil war. And if you can do that, you can do anything.

2 Harry & Meghan

What do Jeremy Clarkson and Piers Morgan have in common? One theory is that they're actually the same person which is why they hated each other for years and had a punch-up in public.[30] In English terms they're sort of the same social type – what people used to call the 'public-school proletariat'. Or sub-Sloane, middle-class men with more than a dash of Sloane but not the whole nine yards. They've both got some of the basic style and RPosh sound which could've helped them end up in the Royal Enclosure, with enough enabling money and the right career path – City, law, Tory politics etc. If that was exactly what they'd wanted – or had the skills for.

You might imagine they've got similar taste in clothes and places to live. Piers is Home Counties, with a posh-sounding name and a smidge of private schooling. Clarkson is from Doncaster but went to Radley, financed by his parents' Paddington Bear toy franchise. Clarkson is a significantly big bloke (at least six foot four) and Piers is Big Enough at six foot one-ish. And there's a somewhat army connection with Piers and an army-admiring one for Jeremy.

Another thing about their education is the amount of it they got. In a period when the parents of middle-class boomers stage II – Clarkson is the older by almost five years – were starting to assume university or at least some sort of recognised higher education was essential for their darlings, they didn't get it. Clarkson failed most of his A-levels ("I got a C and two Us, and I have a Mercedes Benz").[31] Piers got an A in English, a B in history and a C in French,[32] which would've done it, but he didn't go. So by then they wouldn't have been obvious recruits for top metropolitan liberal elite gigs i.e. the *Economist*, the *FT* or the broadsheets, or the BBC serious news ranks. Instead they started in local journalism and got into the London tabloid world in its most infamous Golden Age, when people would take a chance on bold boys who had the makings of a public personality in them.

And they've both done terribly well: money wise, personal brand wise, TV wise. They both have great deals with Rupert Murdoch – Morgan's, assuming it's still going (there've been some tricky moments), has to be the best ever for a UK-based TV journalist/presenter. Apparently it's worth £50 million over three years and it's syndicated round Murdoch platforms in the US (Fox News) and in Australia (Sky News Australia). Morgan has taken his Talk TV (the channel's closing down) spot taking *Piers Morgan Uncensored*, to YouTube, but he's not left Murdoch altogether.

In 1999 he famously said, "I've always made it a strict rule in life to ingratiate myself with three categories of people: newspaper owners, potential newspaper owners and billionaires. And since Mohamed Al-Fayed is a billionaire and would love to own a newspaper, sucking up to him seems an extremely sensible move."[33] Clarkson has a weekly column in the *Sunday Times* and one in the *Sun*, and a deal with Amazon Prime to make *Clarkson's Farm*. In 2014 he famously earned £14 million – huge by British TV standards.

They're both 'Conservative', but not active politicians, let alone policy wonks. They're both friends of David Cameron. Clarkson lives in Oxfordshire and was once reckoned to be part of the wider Chipping Norton set when it ruled the world. Equally importantly, they're both besties of Rebekah Brooks, chief executive of News UK.

Oh, and they both sound as if they *hate* – I mean absolutely put your reputation on the line about it – Meghan Markle, Duchess of Sussex, wife of Prince Harry. On 16 December 2022 Jeremy Clarkson wrote in the *Sun* that he lies awake at night "dreaming of the day Meghan is paraded naked through the streets of every town in Britain while the crowd chants 'Shame' and throws lumps of excrement at her". It provoked more than 25,000 complaints – the highest number the Independent Press Standards Organisation (IPSO) ever received – and a lot of coverage, most of it saying this was no way to treat a woman whatever she's like. The Duchess herself complained. After which Clarkson tweeted a sort of smirky, not-really apology – "I've rather put my foot in it".[34] But Murdoch didn't let him go.

What exactly had provoked him to it? In *Grazia Daily* Georgia Aspinall describes the story behind Jeremy Clarkson's strange obsession with Meghan Markle.[35] She compares it to Piers Morgan's use of it as a marketing tactic – older men clinging to relevance by attacking her. Before his infamous piece in the *Sun*, according to Aspinall, Clarkson had publicly attacked Markle seven times on his various press and TV platforms. There wasn't any evidence that they'd ever met, she said, let alone that he had hopes of a friendship or more.

What he said – until the viral *Sun* piece – simply reflected the tabloid consensus that Megan is manipulative, insincere, hypocritical and a Californian actress and therefore a danger to the monarchy, the nation and world peace. But it got Clarkson the attention he and his platform needed.

Neither Morgan nor Clarkson is what you'd call an analytical media intellectual, but they both know what they're there to do. The thing that matters in their life is having to command attention. Be clickbait, go viral. And they have to please the Big Man. It's the same Big Man in both their cases: Rupert Murdoch. And they both know that the rich and powerful in the UK national press don't like – really, really, don't like – what the alleged dimwit Prince Harry is doing with his risk-taking actions against the UK press. This is something *all* Fleet Street is unanimous about. They're all thinking 'we could be next' – someone with money/backing/whatever could be emboldened by Harry to take them on. They like to call these challenges threats to Press Freedom but the real threats to that come in the form of the global super-rich using the libel litigation called SLAPPS[36] to shut up journalists who publish disobliging but true and important things about them – crucial examples here are the various legal actions from the rich Brexit-backing Arron Banks against the *Guardian*'s Carol Cadwalladr.[37]

On 9 March 2021, Piers Morgan walked out of the live ITV show he anchored, *Good Morning Britain*, having said of Meghan Markle the day before, "I don't believe a word she says" (when talking to Oprah about her suicidal thoughts). He was challenged by his *Good Morning Britain* colleague, weatherman Alex Beresford, who, like Meghan Markle, is mixed race. It looked very snowflaky at the time (in the sense of dishing it out, but not taking it). There were 41,015 complaints to the regulator Ofcom and Dame Carolyn McCall, CEO of ITV, took the Duchess's side. Morgan stayed out of ITV to some considerable advantage because he went back to Murdoch and the fabulous TV contract whereas he'd had to manage on just £1.1 million pa at ITV.

Some of the backstory filtered out, particularly in an inspired bit of digging by Kim Renfro and Lauren Edmonds from Business Insider,[38] which showed that Morgan and the Duchess had known each other for some time. They'd had a number of jolly meetings, after which he'd written some very positive things about her (the implication of the piece seems to be he'd even been a bit sweet on her).[39] But after she cut him and he wasn't invited to the royal wedding, while other people in his all-purpose celebrity world were, he turned increasingly nasty (the Duchess, as it turned out, had had the usual royal comms briefing to be very careful with media people – useful for a rising actress, but dangerous for a royal duchess.) These two saloon bar celebrities claimed to dislike the Duchess for rather similar reasons, saying that she was in fact manipulative and insincere, leaving us to draw the conclusion that that's how most people like her probably were.

Or, to be precise, Californian, which meant she took positions on things, or engaged in what the *Spectator* called 'virtue signalling', or what the world was then coming to call woke. In Tom Bower's book on the Sussexes (and he really didn't like her) he describes how she'd shocked a party of Harry's old muckers by pulling them up about their misogyny and casual racism.[40] They'd concluded that she was an annoying woman with sense of humour failure. The irony here is that, of course, if anyone's entitled to be woke it's an American 'bi-racial' woman. The reality of woke's origins is as a long-standing Black American warning – look out for the racists. In the nation that gave us slavery, lynching and the KKK this had some relevance.

But it was down to the *Sunday Telegraph* editor Allister Heath to spell it out about the Sussexes. Heath, the columnist who famously said on 23 September 2022 that the Liz Truss/Kwasi Kwarteng budget is "a moment in history that will radically transform Britain" set it out right there, about the *political* undertones of anti-Meghanism. He said that *she and by extension the Sussexes, had gone over to rampant leftiness.* It was their betrayal of all we held most dear in favour of Oprah-ism (7 March 2021), and its easy versions of feminism, anti-racism and the rest.

The French-born and part-educated (before the LSE) Allister Heath has become a particularly enthusiastic kind of British patriot. He was ranked 87th in Iain Dale's list of the 'Top 100 most influential people on the Right' in October 2017. In a *Telegraph* piece on 14 December 2022 he describes Harry and Meghan's Netflix "documentary" (Heath's inverted commas!) as an "egregious betrayal of the nation and the Royal Family". Heath talks about "the woke revolutionaries, the hard-left ideological storm-troopers who have taken over so many of our institutions and brainwashed our children". He believed their Netflix documentary "weaponises the anti-Western, anti-British woke ideology for personal gain".[41]

Heath then manages to work in the idea of growing numbers here and abroad being exposed to critical race theory and therefore likely to think that the Sussexes narrative makes sense.[42] To him it's all part of the progressive plot to wean young people away from patriotism and traditional institutions. It's a big charge to make against the Sussexes, and Heath has made it pretty explicit.

These three high-profile rants make it clear that it was actually the Sussexes who were being 'weaponised'. Whatever their strengths and weaknesses – his alleged dimness, her alleged ambition and insincerity, their extraordinary row with the Royal Family (and see the hilarious *South Park* on the Sussexes' "Worldwide Privacy Tour and Prince Harry's autobiography *Waagh*) what really matters is the way they were being framed for the culture wars. For media purposes they were the super-example of all those aristocrats' daughters and plutocrats' or A-list celebrities' sons who'd taken up 'extreme' or left-wing causes, or 'virtue-signalled' their 'luxury beliefs'. The rhetoric's always the same. If people so insanely privileged as this take up a cause, *it must be inherently inauthentic,* because people like this are so not like you, gentle reader, in the God-fearing patriotic provinces (if this sounds overwrought just look at what those papers actually said).

These meta-attacks meant open season for the Fleet Street harridans to do Meghan over – to resource and apparently pay for stories that suggested she was living hell for everyone who worked for her in the various royal set-ups.

They persuaded her estranged dad Thomas Markle quite early on to imply that she'd cut him off since marrying Harry.[43] They constantly compared her to Kate, the good girl with a sense of duty. There is some suggestion that the palace PR machine may have helped frame this particular picture, but that's not the issue. The point is that they were monstered for her liberal/woke/Californian beliefs and he was done over for supporting her. Not only that but for his bold series of lawsuits against newspapers for their invasions of privacy – a sort of Leveson Part Two, after an age in which the newspapers thought they'd seen that threat off by lobbying so effectively to stop the real Leveson Part Two.

As Archie Bland has pointed out in the *Guardian*, Piers Morgan has used a remarkably careful constant form of words in denying that he ever asked anyone to hack a phone.[44] But an increasing number of commentators have come out to say the evidence looks bad for Morgan. The judge in Prince Harry's case against the former Mirror Group Newspapers (now Reach plc), where Morgan was editor of the *Daily Mirror* from 1995 to 2004, was Justice Timothy Fancourt. The *Independent*'s report (15 December 2023) stated, "A High Court judge has accepted evidence that Piers Morgan knew journalists were involved in phone hacking while he was editor of the *Daily Mirror*", which sounded pretty damning.[45] Nonetheless, Morgan has always denied involvement and has never actually been arrested/charged with phone hacking.

The Harry issue couldn't be more real for Piers Morgan. Or for the almost unanimous group of national newspapers who absolutely don't want strong independent regulation. They want to keep the self-regulator IPSO, whose history, like its predecessor the Press Complaints Commission (PCC), is of a notable disinclination to punish almost any members for anything.

The papers' current agreed story about hostile coverage of the Sussexes emerging from their various spokespeople and proxies more recently is simply that *the Sussexes brought it on themselves*. Everyone had loved them and the papers showed it in the early days with very positive coverage. This positivity, so they say, lasted from the earliest days when their story broke, through to the marriage and beyond. The criticism only emerged later as the real story started to slip out in those items, like the one about her treatment of staff. There was no prejudicial/political case against them, and certainly no racism, so this account goes. This official account is undermined, however, by an analysis of newspaper coverage from the earliest days, where a number of hares are set running – the idea, for instance, that Harry is a simple soul easily manipulated by a more experienced woman. A rabbit in the headlights. Our boy had been in some sense kidnapped.

As early as November 2016, Rachel Johnson (sister of Boris), was writing in Mail Online that Meghan Markle had "failed my Mum Test". She had "expertly played the playboy prince". She divorced, and had then dropped her "gorgeous chef boyfriend" like a hot brick. Which for Ms Johnson was "a red line". The Royal Family, she concluded, needed a tremendously limpet-like sticker like Sophie Wessex or Kate Middleton.[46] There's more. The following year Melanie McDonagh in the *Spectator* clarified the view from on high: "Obviously, seventy years ago, Meghan Markle would have been the kind of woman the Prince would have had for a mistress, not a wife".[47]

In an hilarious piece in Buzzfeed News on 13 January 2020, Ellie Hall analyses the individual comparisons between Meghan and Kate and the long list of instances where Meghan is criticised and Kate praised for doing exactly the same thing. They set the stories side by side to make the story watertight.[48] We know this happens but rarely has framing being so forensically framed. So the question of whether the national press was out to get them, and if so, why, becomes more than just business as usual, constructing a dramatic narrative that grips readers and viewers, playing out as teaser headlines and online clickbait. It moves the story into culture wars earlier and more purposefully. It isn't a family drama like *The Crown*, but something more deliberate and more consistent with the papers' positions over time. No one has quite said the Sussexes are cultural Marxists (can you imagine either Meghan or Harry has the faintest grasp of this obscure bit of political history?). But the *Telegraph*'s Heath came very close.

PS: As I researched and wrote about this curious foursome, Harry and Meghan, Jeremy and Piers, I found myself constantly confused between the two titans of comment. I was forever checking my notes about, say, their respective A-level results to make sure I hadn't misplaced or conflated them.

There are obvious differences – JC is famous for *Top Gear* and farming, PM for high-profile interviews at the showbiz edge of politics/social affairs. Clarkson can sometimes be quite funny, but there's never a flicker with Morgan; he's marvellously self-absorbed.

But in addition to my old-world social typology of them as the public school proletariat, there's another newer online characterisation that seems to apply here. I'm nervous of using it, because Tanya Gold, a writer I really like, whether she's talking about food or world wars, says it's a horrible term, snobby, racist, lookist and a lot of other things that hadn't occurred to me...

The fact is I think of them both as... gammons. This isn't a snobby thought for me (anything but) or a particularly Christian one (Jews and Muslims don't eat ham as Tanya Gold points out);[49] rather I think of gammons as confident, incurious members of my own mature middle-class world who look – rightly or wrongly – as if they like a drop and a big dinner. It's because they have that sort of dark, pinky-grey brick colouring. So the gammons are men in late middle age who feel they own the world or ought to. And such is Jeremy Morgan's collective style that they're melded in my imagination as one large lump of British... charcuterie.

3 Farage

In May 2020 Nigel Farage, the original crusader of Brexit and former MEP, found a new job as an unofficial member of the coastguard. It's allowed him to wear the off-duty part of his Home Counties saloon bar Sloane wardrobe. Checked shirts that were Tattershallish. Cheerful scarves at the neck. And I like to imagine the brass-button double-breasted blazer you could reasonably call 'yacht club'. Later that year, he wore colourful shorts and short-sleeved shirts. There is a quality to Farage's wardrobe that Americans – he spends a lot of time there – would consider very English.

Farage has a personal connection with the migrant boats through having a holiday home on the seafront in the village of Dungeness. Indeed, he seems to have spent much, if not most, of the lockdown periods there, rather than at his home near Downe, so he must have witnessed some arrivals almost from his front door. There's also an RNLI station in Dungeness where the lifeboats bring many ashore. He's long been a deep-sea fisherman and liked going out in fishing boats to fish in the middle of the night (amidst all his other activities). This helped develop contacts among the largely pro-Brexit Kentish commercial sea fishermen who have often tipped him off about migrant arrivals.

During lockdown he ventured constantly with an LBC film crew to watch for small boat crossings of asylum seekers from France. Sometimes he even ventured onto a boat himself to get a closer look at the frighteningly frail-looking inflatables, completely packed with people. He said every time that it was terrible and would get worse. And he added, echoing his great friend Donald Trump's electioneering speech of 2015 about Mexican immigrants, some awful warnings about the people who were coming.

The numbers did increase; from May 2020 to December 2023 the yearly numbers rose from 8,466 to 45,755 in 2022 then 29,437 in 2023.[50] There was a dip in 2023 when the government did a deal with Albania to curb arrivals of Albanians by boat, who the UK government asserted were *economic migrants without legitimate asylum claims – something that is difficult to verify.*

Later, after he became the key attraction of the new Fox News-wannabe TV channel GB News in June 2021, Farage continued to talk about illegal immigration. In 2023, when new prime minister Rishi Sunak made 'stopping the boats' one of his five pledges, Farage was dismissive. In 2024 he said the Tories would lose the next election and deserved to because they don't understand the British people's real concerns, meaning immigration.

'The great invasion of the boat people' was a constant in mainstream media and in anger online. Were they criminals, for instance? Or, worse still, Muslim terrorists sent to help existing cells? Whoever they were, it was made clear that they were being put into *hotels* – four-star hotels, so they said – and generously cosseted.

And the locals where they were housed were often upset about it. Sometimes they gathered in small groups of concerned women with hopeless placards. They said they weren't racist, but it wasn't right to bring lots of single young men to family areas like theirs.[51] Sometimes the protesters were angry men, allegedly organised by the English Defence League, former colleagues of Tommy Robinson (Steve Bannon's English hero, whom he called "the backbone of this country").[52] And then there was trouble, because the angry men were looking for it. They often cited grooming gangs in other places as their pretext.

Steve Bannon, Trump's key strategist of 2017, Boris Johnson's secret bestie and coordinator of alt-right political parties across

Europe – the same ones Putin tends to favour – faced prison in 2020. He'd started an initiative to raise money to build the Mexico wall and elicited some $25 million from patriotic Americans eager to help. But it didn't get built, and he and his collaborators were charged with fraud, siphoning off some for themselves in 2020, and found guilty.[53] Bannon faced prison, but on his last day in office, Donald Trump pardoned him. Bannon has shown just how strong a culture war theme an anti-immigration stance could be.

In one violent affair apparently organised by EDL[54] types outside the Suites Hotel in Knowsley, Merseyside, which housed asylum seekers, things got nasty. A police car was set on fire and there were 15 arrests.[55]

People debated whether the government's failure to stop the boats was incompetence or something more deliberate. They certainly made for good television visuals, not unlike the 'build the wall' border between the US and Mexico. Trump – Nigel Farage's bestie, so it seems, never did build that wall with Mexico so the struggle continued and pictures kept coming. Successive Tory home secretaries – Priti Patel, Suella Braverman and James Cleverly – always had the boat people to go back to when there was a thin supply of big stories. Especially if they were making their pitches to lead the next Tory government – whenever that might be. The boat people were a gift that kept on giving.

Nigel Farage had seen a brilliant example of culture wars political campaigning at scale through his time spent with Donald Trump. Their bromance started in 2016, when Farage started appearing at Trump's rallies as his warm-up act. This meant, in turn, he met Trump supporters – very different people from the classic Republican globalist neocons – and learnt about their version of US 'political technology', still years ahead of ours. Farage was a pioneer in the integration of British and American new right-wingers described in Matthew d'Ancona's brilliant essay of 2019, 'Bannon's Britain', which anticipated today's Conservative Party, after Boris Johnson threw the 'one-nation' old guard out of the window and under the bus.[56]

The reality of the UK asylum seekers, when you cruelly reduced them to numbers, was that, however they grew, there were significantly fewer of them coming in than in continental European countries. Germany, France, Spain and even Austria had far larger numbers, and we were at a similar level to Italy. Some smaller European nations took on significantly more, as a proportion of their populations, than we did. It was, and continues to be, an acknowledged world problem, and no one had quite figured out how to solve it. But the boat people mantra is a super useful dead cat story, brilliantly dramatised by Nigel Farage. It was a marvellous metaphor for British resistance. We would fight them on our beaches, especially at Hastings.

But in 2022, Boris Johnson's government conceived a made-for-TV drama so extraordinary that no modern writing room group of young satirists working overtime could ever have invented it. The idea, quite beyond parody, was to take the backlog of unprocessed asylum seekers in the UK and send them to Rwanda in east Africa which was, by all accounts, a very nice place which hadn't had a genocide since 1994. They'd be flown there – up and out – and the processing would be done there. If they were granted asylum, they could stay... there. *But under no circumstances would they be allowed back to the UK.* It was less clear where they'd go if they weren't allowed into Rwanda, but that was their lookout; the cruel gangs who organised the boats at huge profit were to blame anyway.

On closer examination, the spectacular deal with the Rwandan government wasn't exactly the answer it sounded. It was contested at every level, by lawyers working for the migrants, by successively grander judges at home – the Supreme Court said Rwanda was definitely *not* a safe place – and then in Europe, with the ECHR – the European Court of Human Rights – blocking it. Right-wing Brexiteer Tories then said we should leave the ECHR. We hadn't escaped the EU in 2016 to be dictated to by them now, they proclaimed. The facts that the ECHR wasn't part of the EU and Churchill had been one of its founding supporters didn't carry any weigh with the Leavers. The ECHR was foreign and obviously woke.

And then it became clear the whole thing wasn't exactly at scale. Even if they were cleared for take-off – as I write in 2024, when Labour ended the scheme, not a single migrant has been sent to Rwanda – the scheme allowed for, at very most, a few thousand people a year, when there was a backlog of around 50,000 people in those hotels, curious barges and airfield buildings. If the numbers were so small, what was the point? *It was deterrence, so the Conservatives insisted.* A Google search would warn them in their bombed-out towns in Iraq and Syria that they were heading to Rwanda, wherever that was. But the subtext would say it was really a micro-lottery. And the cruel people-traffickers would undoubtedly tell them nobody had actually gone there, and probably nobody would. It didn't sound like much of a deterrent. How could they tell whether it would work? There doesn't seem to be any evidence, and they'd spent £700 million before they'd sent anyone.

There were furious Tory-on-Tory debates. High-profile right-wingers like Lee Anderson MP – by then 'deputy chairman' of the party – resigned about the proposed Rwanda legislation being too soft.[57] And Rishi Sunak's personal ratings plummeted, as it all looked like absolute chaos. There were even critics in the party saying the PM should step down, meaning there'd have been six Tory PMs in the 14 years since 2010, with an election coming up. Where would it all end?

Meanwhile, the spectacular stories – the invasion of the boat people and the mass airborne exit to Rwanda – had done their job, to distract us all from absolutely everything else in the news and tell us that immigrants were dangerous and would steal everything we'd got. And to remind us that at least *some* Tories – and Nigel Farage – were really tough on illegal immigration. They also served to stop people from discussing the vastly greater numbers of non-European legal migrants, huge and growing at a lick now that we didn't have the flow of skilled people from Europe after Brexit. Legal migration to the UK had gone from 572,000 in 2017 to an (estimated) 672,000 for 2023, almost 23 times the coastal invasion (an estimated) 29,437 in 2023.[58] And we called that controlling our borders.

Employers, private and public, were of course desperate for more people to do practically every kind of job here after the pandemic. They bemoaned the huge numbers who had unaccountably left the workforce. The old perception of the Tories as the *party of business* – mainstream CBI-ish, publicly traded companies with familiar names – was changing. The Tories morphed, rather like the Republican party in the US, into the party of individual plutocrats, City mavericks, partners in hedge fund traders and useful populist tokens. Plus, *international* supporters. Boris Johnson had a positive clique of people like that, including a good many super-rich Russians.[59] (But after Ukraine and the shaming of his super-rich hedge fund friend Crispin Odey – with workplace sexual assault allegations – people tended to play all that sort of thing down).

There had been a time when Johnson seemed to be dependent on his rich inner circle – particularly Lord Bamford – for bed and board everywhere. How did he spend it? Where did he develop the expectations that made the £275,000 a year he got from the *Daily Telegraph* for one column a week seem like "chicken feed" to him? After all, it put him well into the top 1% of UK income earners and it was 3.17 times an MP's pay.

Johnson's blingy 21st-century milieux contrasts sharply with the strands of his globally mixed background. His maternal grandfather Sir James Fawcett, a high-minded barrister, had been on the board of the ECHR, the constant enemy of the anti-immigrant Tories, for 22 years and its president for 9 of them.[60] Johnson's sister Rachel had a smart running joke about her father Stanley being constantly attracted to left-wing women.

4 Defund the BBC

Defund the BBC,[61] one of the most interesting engagements in the UK's recent culture wars, appeared to emerge literally overnight. It was launched on Twitter (now X) one Sunday evening in June 2020 by James Yucel, a first-year Glasgow University student, in his room. His manifesto was basically "We've got one aim and that aim is to ultimately scrap the BBC licence fee".[62]

The next morning there it was, having garnered 20,000 followers, an enthusiastic article in the *Daily Express* and an admiring interview on Rupert Murdoch's Talk Radio, with a piece in the *Sun* by the same interviewer, Dan Wootton, the paper's executive editor. (Wootton was later to become famous as GB News' lead presenter – and for the extraordinary allegations about him by in *Byline Times*. A pair of former *Sun* colleagues claimed that Wootton in effect ran a sort of blackmail ring among former colleagues and minor celebrities based on secret filming. Wootton was put 'on suspension' by GB News in September 2023, then actually dismissed in March 2024.)[63]

Yucel joined the Westmonster News podcast the following morning. Westmonster was founded by Arron Banks, Nigel Farage's collaborator and the UK's then largest-ever political donor (to 'Leave EU').

By that Thursday, @DefundBBC had 62,000 followers on Twitter. James Yucel, 18 at the time, said, "I didn't expect it to go big... I'm just a kid with a laptop frustrated at the way the BBC conduct themselves".[64] Some things about this apparently picture perfect campaign struck seasoned media analysts as having the signs of a coordinated initiative rather than being just a happy accident. *It sounded like astroturf* – that wonderful American word for an ostensibly 'grassroots' campaign that turns out to have been organised by political campaigning professionals, usually in Washington or London. Two kinds of analysis followed. First, Professor Steven Barnett and Dr Doug Specht at Westminster University looked at the patterns of #DefundtheBBC's online support.[65] Then journalists looked at Master Yucel himself and the hardened professionals gathered around him to create the organisation.

The online analysis was fascinating. Many of Defund the BBC's enthusiasts were anonymous – including one who tagged it nearly 150 times – making it hard to tell who they really were, and some showed 'bot' characteristics, which they defined as:

- Accounts which lack personal information. E.g. no profile picture, a handle that contains strings of number etc.
- Accounts with little or no followers
- Accounts set up shortly before they start producing large qualities of messages about a given topic
- Accounts that post repetitive messages and/or give vague generic responses
- Accounts with suspicious response rates or frequency of posting e.g. too quick or frequent
- Accounts that are mostly reposting from accounts that also fall into having bot characteristics as above.

Their concerns and enthusiasms were indicative. Many, according to the Barnett and Specht report in The Conversation, were supporters of Tommy Robinson and other right-wing heroes. Among those who piled in were the actor turned right-wing politician Laurence Fox and 'classic liberal' YouTuber Mahyar Tousi.

The writers pointed out that the vast majority of campaign followers, judging by their Twitter history, were committed

Brexiteers and followers of the Leave campaign, which itself has a long history of hostility towards the BBC. They concluded that their initial suspicions had been borne out: "from the very beginning the campaign wanted to look like a spontaneous eruption of popular anger. In practice, it looks like a suspiciously coordinated operation, linking together several pro-Brexit, free-market (and in a few cases far-right) social media accounts... to what extent is this another confected media campaign in the long-running culture war against the BBC?"

It didn't take much to establish that Master Yucel was, in fact, a precocious and sophisticated young Conservative whose links went way outside student politics. He was treasurer of Glasgow University Conservatives and Unionist Association[66] and earlier that year he had published an article about how to increase Conservative representation in universities on the hard-right Free-Market Conservatives website.[67] Earlier still, just before the 2019 election, he'd written a detailed analysis of the DUP's likely post-election strategy in the Glasgow University student newspaper the *Glasgow Guardian.*[68] But there was lots more; just days before launching Defund the BBC, Yucel had been working as an intern for his local Conservative MP Tom Hunt, voted in for Ipswich in the December 2019 election.[69] Hunt was a member of the hard-Brexit-supporting ERG group of Tory MPs.

Yucel's stint in Westminster doing Hunt's comms – picked up by the Zelo Street website – will have made him connections which helped make the London media follow-through so swift and seamless.[70]

By mid-July, Yucel had raised £30,000 in donations from just 125 people, an average of £240 per person.[71] That was 50% more than the TV licence fee and seemed implausibly high for a real grassroots campaign without some big backers. Defund the BBC had an official launch with this funding, according to their eager supporter the Guido Fawkes right-wing site Order Order: "They have brought in campaign experience from the group behind 'Stand up for Brexit' and will be working with MPs and other big names like Darren

Grimes... Defund the BBC is turning the momentum they found online into a targeted campaign... Defund the BBC could be one to watch."[72]

The *New European*'s Steve Anglesey took up the story of the campaign at the end of July, describing the billboard DTB put up in mid-July on "one of the busiest roads in London".[73] It featured two of the BBC presenters the right most loved to hate, Gary Lineker and Emily Maitlis (then fronting *Newsnight*) along with their BBC salaries: £1.75 million per annum and £260,000 per annum respectively. The headline message was "Are you still paying?"

#DefundtheBBC's precise staffing – like many of the pressure groups and fronts emerging from the young new right-wing Conservative post-Brexit world – was sometimes unclear. Anglesey identified Liam Deacon as the press officer, a key role in this kind of media-based initiative. Deacon had worked as press officer on the Brexit Party's 2019 general election campaign and before that at the American alt-right import Breitbart London, former home of Steve Bannon. According to Anglesey, in the 14 months before the referendum, Deacon had published 450 stories about immigration, migrants or Islam. Other Defund the BBC 'champions' included Darren Grimes, famous for hosting the "so many damn Blacks" interview that wrecked David Starkey's mainstream media career. Yet another was the interesting former GB News contributor, the dog-collared Calvin Robinson – ordained by an obscure historic faith – who has been fired for his support of Laurence Fox on that station. Robinson said, "The BBC seems to have become an outlet for woke propaganda." Defund the BBC's 'campaign coordinator', Rebecca Ryan, turned out to be a veteran of Stand up for Brexit. Everything linked back to the Brexit people. Defund the BBC could often be traced back to 55 Tufton Street, the multiple political brand owner of the UK's New Right, originally set up by Matthew Elliott in 2009. In that sense, it seemed more like an *initiative* of the movement rather than a separate organisation, let alone a grassroots initiative of a student in his room.

But Defund the BBC morphed over time into a media-friendly

quote machine run by Rebecca Ryan, who turns out regularly for the new generation of right-wing media, conjured up post-Brexit and especially during the pandemic. GB News (first broadcast in June 2021) and Talk TV (started up in April 2022) always had a chair for the rather unimpressive Ryan. She also came up with Defund the BBC's creation myth, with its backstory that the BBC had reported the Black Lives Matter London demonstrations in a shockingly biased way by failing to cover the demonstrators' violence. She would then bang on about the 'liberal elite' in London and Brighton and similar places where the BBC still had audiences. She was conveniently there to tell Talk TV's Jeremy Kyle (remember him?) the story of the BBC's former lead news presenter Huw Edwards paying thousands for explicit sex pictures – told you about the BBC[74] – and to remind viewers that the BBC had once employed Jimmy Savile (actually in the last century).[75] Rebecca Ryan seemed to be a holding operation housed in a cupboard somewhere.

But Defund the BBC had also inspired YouTube channels like ChilliJonCarne, where the basic message about ditching the BBC licence fee – nationally and individually – was played out by a supporter admittedly shy of revealing his real name. His YouTube channel dramatised the idea of your gran being sent to prison for non-payment (watch this channel and have your heart tugged).

Defund the BBC had done its job, which, like all astroturf organisations, was to convince people that unpopular/minority views were very widely shared by people like you. And, more than that, it showed people how to get out of paying the licence fee – there's now a host of sites and channels to tell you just that. It was something for the new gang of Brexit Brothers to do, and by then they'd got a lot of practice.

There's an interesting coda to this story. In his biography attached to his new job description on housing lobby PricedOut's website, James Yucel says he is a "fellow" of the Mercatus Center at George Mason University. It struck me that I'd seen several mentions of this otherwise obscure university recently, so I checked it out. The Mercatus Center at George Mason University – a media-friendly fully funded US public university – is either an integrated part of the university on whose campus it's located and whose reputation for an academic approach and peer-reviewed impartiality it benefits from – or it isn't, depending on who's describing it. The university itself seems to say it's a co-located separate institution, while the Mercatus people say it's closer than that.

Mercatus, however, is separately – privately – funded from the university and appears to operate like a libertarian free-market think tank of the Washington or Westminster kind with lobbying at its core. Originally housed at Rutgers University, it moved to George Mason in the mid-1980s after the Koch family – remember them? – gave the university more than $30 million. The Mercatus Board as at June 2020 included both Charles G. Koch (the surviving Koch brother) and Richard Fink, the former executive vice-president of Koch Industries. How exactly did this former 'student in his room' move into the global Koch orbit?

5 Everyone Loves the National Trust

Everyone loves the National Trust. Well, almost everyone. It saves things for the nation and, historically, it's saved a particular idea of the nation. It looks after beautiful things and provides the nicest possible places for cream teas. There's something for everyone – inside in grand old houses, and outside in glorious landscapes. And just when you're thinking its altogether too toff-worshipping and obsessed with England's rural dreaming, it acquires things like John Lennon's and Paul McCartney's childhood homes and sets zero carbon targets for its acres and its investments.

This is love at scale. The National Trust is the UK's *largest* charity in terms of membership – 5.37 million – and income – £681.9m in 2022–3. It also looks after more acres than anyone except for the Forestry Commission, the MOD and the Crown Estate. It cares for over 250,000 hectares of farmland (over 617,000 acres) and over 780 miles of coastline.

The National Trust owns masses of British history, in terms of houses and gardens, furniture and paintings and every kind of delicious historic collection that you can actually go and see, open to the public. They do research about the history of people and things and explain it all in careful, understandable ways.

People like it for all the things it's *not*. It's not private and privileged. Like the BBC – you can say that it belongs to us. It's not exploitative and profit gouging. It's not governmental or 'party political'. And it's concerned not to be carboniferous at all. It's like its members, mainly mature, concerned middle-class types, in line with the gradual liberalisation of the nation shown in British social attitudes research.

Historically, criticism of the Trust came from people who said it was altogether too deferential and toff loving, that they didn't recognise the modern world or the urban world and weren't keen to maintain the houses and gardens of more *modest* people. And, later, more diverse people. They were mainly promoting what's been called the 'mansion experience' – a touch of the Downton Abbeys – and that audience was declining. And there have been battles over hunting on National Trust land (they don't allow it now).

One way and another the National Trust is in the 'heritage' business – in *show and tell*. And in the *environmental* business, thinking and talking about how to save their world, responding cautiously to new ideas and testing out approaches that might save what they've got for centuries more. Actually, they're said to have been originally rather slow to examine the deeper, more difficult histories of their houses and acres by the lights of their peers in heritage-land, museums, galleries and academia, rather than wildly woke.

But recently the Trust has looked at the history and economics of some of those grand houses in a new way. In a report published in September 2020, they looked at their connections with colonialism and slavery. There were a fair few links – 93 in houses and estates. The connections included Winston Churchill's house, Chartwell in Kent, because of his role of secretary of state for the colonies in the 1920s and his involvement in the Anglo-Irish Treaty of 1921 which led to partition. And his opposition to dominion status for India. It generated almost as much criticism as statue-toppling. Oliver Dowden, the then culture secretary, said the Trust was making (Churchill) a "subject of criticism and controversy".

That did it. An organisation called Restore Trust, founded in 2021, claimed it represented thousands of current or ex-members of the Trust alienated by all this wokeness (just how many supporters they've had is unclear because, unlike the Trust itself, they're not a membership organisation). Restore Trust campaigned relentlessly against the Trust's management *on the contradictory grounds* that they were both too modishly woke and driven by philistine management speak. For the last four years, Restore Trust has campaigned to get the thinking members to vote for their nominees for the NT's Advisory Council.

Their catalogue of complaints was set out in Restore Trust's *very* professional communications, organised by a top PR, Neil Bennett, who'd been City editor of the *Sunday Telegraph*.[76] The charges were that:

- the report on National Trust houses' links to colonialism and slavery and slavery was inspired by woke motives from the Black Lives Matter organisation
- volunteers were pestered into 'inclusiveness' training and other wokery
- Clandon Park – the 18th-century mansion that burnt down in 2015 – has not been restored
- vulgar marketing strategies were being considered to drive turnover.[77]

There was more, but these were the main charges.[78]

The fascinating thing about Restore Trust was that the closer you looked, the more like astroturf it seemed. That's not to say everyone involved was a conscious culture warrior looking to push the 'liberal elite' story in a bad faith playbook way. There were fogeys of all ages who really thought the Trust had dumbed-down things they cared about, like the labelling of exhibits. They also suggested there was altogether too much emphasis on cream teas and a good day out rather than scholarship and safekeeping. Or that they didn't like the paint colours in the restorations (we all care passionately about paint colours now).

But this was different. It was organised and *political*. And the people who were doing the organisation, so it seemed, were politicians with a predictable roster of sympathies and interests. Restore Trust attributed everything they didn't like about the

Trust to an alleged 'political takeover' of the higher management by a group of people who, so they said, had ignored their original mission for the modish woke new priorities These included inclusiveness training, LGBT support (some Pride lanyards somewhere apparently) and all that new research into who former owners were and where their money came from. Not surprisingly, they said the research about particular houses was seriously flawed (could they have got it wrong about all 93 of them?).

But if that that was all true, how did everything still get done? You can't ignore those houses and acres and just write woke strategies all day long. And why did the huge membership numbers rise after the pandemic? The criticism sounded very much like the right's standard playbook of anecdotes about wokeness (otherwise cultural Marxism!).

But ironically, Restore Trust's connections are as easy to follow as their complaints and their actual supporters are difficult to quantify. The whole thing traces back to a cluster of right-wing think tanks in Westminster, starting – you've guessed it – with the 55 Tufton Street group and turning the corner into 2 Lord North Street and the IEA, granddaddy of the world's right-wing think tank network.

At 25, Zewditu Gebreyohanes, Restore Trust's director (until their recent fourth failure to storm the National Trust's Advisory Board), has an impressive backstory. It takes in the late Sir Roger Scruton, patron saint of right-wing fogeys as her university mentor. She worked at one of the right-wing conservatives' favourite think tanks – Policy Exchange – on a history project titled 'Protecting local heritage' (it involved opposing the Churchill College criticisms). She's currently a 'senior researcher' at the Legatum Institute, another right-wing think tank set up and part funded by the Dubai-based Legatum Group, *part owners of GB News* as we saw earlier.[79]

She's also a Conservative government-appointed non-executive director on the board of the V&A. She was appointed by the Department of Culture, Media and Sport (DCMS) when Nadine Dorries was secretary of state. And she spoke at the National

Conservatism Conference in 2023, a clear statement of political sympathies (always follow the links).

Zewditu Gebreyohanes was recently interviewed by the former UKIP deputy leader Peter Whittle, director of the right-wing pressure group New Culture Forum, on its YouTube channel (its mission is to counter the new orthodoxy they say has taken over the cultural sector, *and it's based at 55 Tufton Street*). She complained to the very sympathetic Whittle that people said Restore Trust was 'right wing', whereas it was, she suggested, just a group of disgruntled members who wanted to get the Trust back to its so-called traditional priorities.

The finance tycoon Neil Record is a key founder and board member of Restore Trust. Record, the founder, former chair and largest shareholder in Record Currency Management, was chairman of the global daddy of all opaquely funded right-wing think tanks,[80] the Institute of Economic Affairs (IEA), until July last year.[81] Significantly, Record has also been an important supporter of the Global Warming Policy Foundation think tank, the climate change sceptic group founded in 2009 – and also based in 55 Tufton Street (it's the home of a positive flotilla of right-wing think tanks and pressure groups).[82] The key people in Restore Trust and their supporters aren't comfortable and provincial; they're major Westminster players.

Record is typical of a new group of political activists – the 'pluto-populists', a group adored by Boris Johnson and Liz Truss. Pluto-populists are very rich people, based either in City finance, most typically as hedge fund traders like Sir Paul Marshall (funder of *UnHerd* magazine, part owner of GB News, and allegedly bidding to buy the Telegraph Group) or as owners/controlling shareholders of their businesses. *They can do what they like with their money,* including backing causes that conventional company boards would avoid as too political. (More 'mainstream' business, according to a recent poll, now sees the Labour Party as 'the party of business'.)[83]

Restore Trust has friends in predictable places. *The Spectator* of course and masses in the *Telegraph*. And, as it turned out, Nigel

Farage. Mr Farage said recently in a GB News interview on his programme about the National Trust with the chair of Restore Trust, Cornelia van der Poll, that the NT's gone 'too woke, too PC, lost sight of its original purpose' and 'I hope Restore Trust knocks a bit of common sense back into what was the great National Trust'.

All this poses the fascinating question as to why such a posh/ plutocratic, well-funded and well-connected right-wing special force has chosen to wade in to the affairs of the National Trust. There are undoubtedly real tensions at the Trust anyway – between fogeys and 'modernisers' and between the older and younger more 'liberal' cohorts of members. People who still want the 'mansion experience' and people who'll want something different in future. These are all issues that work their way out as a 126-year-old organisation renegotiates its relationship to a changing world.

But there were some special factors at play here. Normally, the Westminster right-wing lobby worked through its important links with government; the Conservative DCMS had always listened to people who wanted to defund and demoralise the BBC – and they'd been able to act on it, with licence fee freezes and threats of worse. It was the same with arts institutions that received significant amounts of public money. But they couldn't do that to the Trust because it's a charity with its own endowment and a huge membership.

So, to exert pressure, *they needed to get inside*. And that needed an initiative like this. Whatever the Trust's internal debate, it's clear that Restore Trust isn't exactly *grassroots*.

And what is it about the National Trust that warrants such an effort? Of course, the wider Westminster culture wars alliance would love to take such a high-profile cultural scalp and say they've beaten the liberal elite (the cultural Marxists even)! Farage and Suella Braverman would have applauded them. But there's something else. As a huge landowner, its example as an environmentalist could be influential – like the King's. If the hugely trusted – as the polls constantly show it – National Trust speaks for 'zero carbon' by 2030, and speaks against fracking, you might think that important climate change sceptics like Neil Record and his circle could just feel they warranted a change of direction. Neil Record is said to have been a major source of Restore Trust's most current war chest. Will he think it's worth another go?

CONSPIRACY THEORIES
for Profit & Pleasure

HOW TO MILK IT DRY

ANDREW TATE
My Struggle

my Flashy-Washy!

LOVE

MR 24

6 Russell Brand

On 16 September 2023, the *Times* reported an investigation they'd conducted with Channel 4's *Dispatches*. In the article four women accused the actor/comedian/social media personality Russell Brand of a number of offences against them between 2006 and 2013, when he was at the high point of his fame.[84] *Dispatches* made an hour-long programme with his accusers, broadcast on the same Saturday. YouTube, where Brand had a huge international following for his channel, about 6.6 million subscribers, 'demonetised' him on 19 September 2023. He moved his new productions to Rumble, a right-wing US site which hosted and boasted big online people like Sean Hannity, Joe Rogan and Andrew Tate.[85]

After that, Brand became a professional alt-right martyr. He said 'dark forces' from the Establishment were trying to shut him up. *The Times*, *Sunday Times* and C4 were mainstream media (MSM), which had its own agenda, creating false narratives on behalf of that Establishment cabal. Martyrs like Brand are absolutely everywhere now, right-wing populist types on platforms with mikes and TV cameras stuck in their faces saying, without irony, that they're being silenced, cancelled and smeared. The works!

Dan Wootton, the GB News presenter, said something of the kind after *Byline Times*' jaw-dropping story about his private life emerged in relentless detail, issue by issue in 2023:[86]

"There are dark forces out to try and take this brilliant channel down... because GB News is the biggest threat to the establishment in decades, and they will stop at nothing to destroy us."
– 19 July 2023 [87]

But what exactly was this Establishment they were always banging on about? Or indeed anyone else that Brand talks about now in his fanciful street fighting man cult leader language?

Over the eight years from 2015 – when Brand endorsed Labour leader Ed Miliband in the general election – to 2023, Brand's YouTube channel, which started in 2007, had moved from the left to the far right at increasing speed. Over the period, he interviewed Alex Jones, the hysterical American conspiracy theorist; Jordan Peterson, the Canadian right-wing very public intellectual; Tucker Carlson, the former Fox News lead presenter sacked in the aftermath of Dominion Voting Machines' successful case against Fox; and every other alt-right favourite you can think of. He couldn't have picked a higher-profile set of MAGA favourites, almost all of them American.[88]

On the BBC's *Sunday Politics* on 9 June 2013, that well-known leftie Andrew Neil had described Alex Jones as the maddest person they'd ever interviewed. "We have an idiot on the programme today!"[89] In October 2022 a group of parents bereaved at a mass school shooting in Sandy Hook, Connecticut had sued Jones successfully for $965 million for claiming the whole thing was a 'hoax', enacted by 'crisis actors'. His story was that it'd been conjured up by the liberal gun control lobby.

It was very different when Russell Brand interviewed Jones in November 2023. Brand introduced Jones with his characteristic fast-talking hand-waving soapbox word salad. He said, "I invite you to take a different perspective on Alex Jones, an extraordinary talent." And he went on to talk about "the number of times Alex Jones has been right". He didn't mention when he'd been catastrophically wrong, subjecting those Sandy Hook parents to years of crazed trolling. In 2023 US YouTuber Vaush said that Brand's look is 'cult Leader'. He never actually says anything directly but launders right-wing conspiracies with vaguely left-wing populist rhetoric. He seems closer to neo-Nazi than he is anything else.[90]

Over the course of Brand's more recent videos, every conspiracy theory popular in ultra-right America was trailed. He was saying, in effect, that the world you saw was an illusion, rather like *The Truman Show*. It sounded as if he wanted you to doubt the real world. He described all legacy media/the MSM – as Donald Trump did – as fake news. He was equally fawning and uncritical with his other right-wing interviewees, talking them up in his pretentious mystical babble. This meant burning his boats in most of Britain with a view to a pay-off in American MAGA-world. It worked in its way because when the *Times'* accusations came out, Brand was roundly endorsed and supported by his new friends Ben Shapiro, Alex Jones and Andrew Tate (the hyper-misogynistic bodybuilder arrested in Romania for trafficking women – your teenage son will know who he is). Tate said: "Welcome to the club, Russell Brand."[91] What exactly was the club?

I clocked Russell Brand relatively early on TV – not the comedy circuit – because I'd been obsessed with the first few series of *Big Brother* on Channel 4 – watching it and its various spin-offs including *Big Brother's Big Mouth*, where Brand started in 2004, far into the night. It was clearly a new kind of TV, starting in 2000, a precursor of a new kind of 21st-century media world to come. I didn't know where Brand was at or where he came from, but he was clearly singular and *hyper*. He had a pirate/cult leader *look* and a way with words – fanciful, whimsical, archaic, mock-heroic – and a big vocabulary which endeared him to wordy people. And he had a funny voice, unplaceable in the standard range; it often sounded rather camp, but it wasn't that either, though, combined with his extravagant hair and panto get-ups, a fair few viewers will have taken those cues. But when you saw him talking to women that clearly wasn't it. They often seemed mesmerised by him and *confused*. And he stared at them fixedly.

He seemed to know then – in his late twenties – the power he had and what he could get away with, but you couldn't see exactly what the master plan might be or where that spooky confidence came from.

A few series did it for me with *Big Brother*. I never watched it after 2005 though it played out on C4 till 2010. And I forgot about Brand. The big world didn't, however, and he was in American films by 2008, starring with Jonah Hill, Jennifer Garner – even Tom Cruise. He became a Brit export to Hollywood and married Katy Perry. I didn't see any of his big films – they included *Get Him to the Greek* (2010), *Rock of Ages* (2012) and *Arthur* (2011). They weren't rated as *that good* and nobody seemed to think it was the end of the world when he all but stopped making them.

Back then Brand was in the world of occasional British talk show fly-in appearances – Graham Norton and Jonathan Ross – saying the occasional interesting thing but actually lost to us, so I thought.

Let's forget, for one moment, the issue that's coming up next, the silly but unpleasant moment with Jonathan Ross and Andrew Sachs's granddaughter in 2008 – it should've been a clue about Brand's character; nonetheless I didn't much care at the time. However, it did mean he left the BBC, and so did Ross.

What I wasn't prepared for – in 2014 – was how Brand suddenly became a luvvie of the Left – the quite *soft left*, one has to say, and the endorser of Ed Miliband for the 2015 general election.[92] And he did books – terribly successful and presumably money-making ones by old world pre-online subscription publishing standards. Everyone said they loved him. He was the *Guardian*'s Owen Jones' new bestie – check them out when they were a barnstorming duo for huge liberal audiences in huge buildings and screened in cinemas around the country.[93] Even clever George Monbiot said he was "the best thing that had happened to the left in years" (he's admitted to regretting it since). The point seemed to be that he was a new kind of left-wing person who connected to the young. And a repenting sinner too, open about the drugged-up, sexed-up life he'd lived. And one of his books was even called *Revolution* (2014).

I found this period more than usually irritating, I should say, but I was never exactly a fan anyway. And I thought he was using his new 'influencer' power in a rather calculating way with his impressionable leftist audience who seemed clueless about how opportunistic poseurs like Brand operated. A woman I know told me that she found him – just from the TV – simultaneously frightening, "sex on legs" *and* confusing. She didn't like him but she couldn't look away.

It was a quite different response from what your average polite Hollywood sex god provoked – more 70s rockstar. But, like Mick Jagger and his 'audience' with star-struck establishment types in 1967, he was mixing it with big people about big issues representing youth (he was 39 by then). I lost interest again quickly.

I was back by 2020. By then I'd long had a mega YouTube habit, hours spent watching everything from high politics to low gossip and every kind of medical scare. So it was inevitable that the clickbait titles on Russell Brand's channel – which already had incredible numbers – would draw me in. There were all kinds of conspiracy theories being *trailed* – rather cunningly – but not always completely *owned*. And a long list of very right-wing interviewees.

I recognised a lot of the themes and memes. I already knew that New Agey and 'wellness' types of all ages had rapidly become anti-vaxxers and anti-lockdowners during the pandemic, and they were already bristling with hostility towards *bigness* generally (Big Government, Big Pharma). And I'd come to the unkind conclusion that if you're capable of believing one set of impossible things before breakfast then you're a sitting duck for all those stories about the Establishment wanting total Orwellian control – you'll be alt-right by Christmas.

But I hadn't realised how much sooner Brand had come to this conclusion than me. Here he was, talking to everyone from Alex Jones to Jordan Peterson and regularly dissing the Democrats (clearly that huge audience was mainly in America) and saying Trump – whatever you thought of him – *might just have got it right about some things*. I'd been sunk in the culture wars vocabulary, the people, the memes, the frogs, the lot since 2010, so I realised that Brand had moved very seriously to the right.[94] There he was, regaining *relevance*, a big American audience and big money just by setting up a production company with the studio in a sort of garden shed in Oxfordshire and going along with the talking points. He could go where he wanted, so it seemed, near totally under the mainstream media radar. He was saying everything his 2014 thoughtful fans would've hated to everyone they would've hated – but they didn't seem to have noticed. Then came the *Sunday Times*/Channel Four story and absolutely everything changed.

Over the course of his YouTube channel's schedule it was clear that Brand had evolved a sort of windy cover story about what he was doing. As someone who had been a vocal critic of the Establishment/deep state/mainstream media and the rest of them, he said, in effect, he'd found a surprising fellow-feeling for right-wing populists about the corrupt Establishment. Maybe they should discuss things and reach a way to work together and save humankind – cutting out the hopelessly compromised old-style middlemen. But the people he talked to and talked up were by then absolute pariahs – sobs! – everywhere in his old 2015 UK fanbase. So you wondered who exactly the cover story was designed for.

There were a number of explanations for Brand's very sharp right turn. One, put forward by Peter Guest in *Wired*, was that the 'dark economics' of the YouTube algorithm meant he responded to whatever brought in the audience and the money. It was all about 'engagement' – and conspiracy stories and alt-right celebrities got you that.[95]

Some cynics say Brand knew by around 2018 that the sex stories would be coming out eventually and he needed more than just expensive lawyers for protection. Like Trump he needed the power of martyrdom, the idea that he spoke up for his audience and so The Power was persecuting him for that, but his base loved him for it. Others have another more paranoid-sounding explanation; they believe Brand was in some way *recruited* in the odd years after the referendum, brought in by a shadowy alt-right team who'd headhunted an impressive group of social influencers with promises of status and a world stage along with quite extraordinary returns.

No one is quite sure how to put this idea. It can sound conspiratorial after all; it's difficult for people who are constantly mocking QAnon and the Great Replacement theory. What critics do point out, however, is the apparent pay trajectory that parallels the move any influencer makes from left to right. The big platforms – from major newspapers and conferences to speaking at £2,000- a-plate dinners – all take you up. The world of hyper-funded think tanks throws its doors open wide to conspiracy theorists and right-wing celebrities on the circuit. (Brand is like, say, the controversial cross-bench peer Baroness Fox of Buckley who constantly says she is 'left wing' – whatever that means – while always walking and talking like a right-wing duck to other right-wing ducks in right-wing venues.) When Brand's on right-wing platforms he constantly says that *everything needs to go*, so that's his cover for getting together with what Thomas Frank calls "the Wrecking Crew". As Steve Bannon famously described his comms strategy "flood the zone with shit", so people get disoriented and are prepared to believe absolutely *anything*.[96] At that point, so the thinking goes, they're ready for authoritarians – strong men. There seems to be something to this.

In an offering from his new Rumble channel (part owned by the rightist billionaire Peter Thiel) Brand was celebrating Trump's January Iowa victory, saying how his speech was a positive triumph of civility and conflict resolution.[97] Brand must know perfectly well that if there's a US civil war it'll be because Trump persists with his big lie about the 2020 election. And that if Trump wins, Ukraine loses. The Western European leaders – plus the UK's new Labour government – will be desperately planning together for the consequences. We know – because they've both said it so often – that Trump is a long-term flabby fanboy for Putin, who, understandably, goes along with it and flatters him. Russell Brand must know all this – how could he not – but he knows his audience and his new peer group even better.

And he wants to keep his rebel cult leader status, even though his life must by now be run by accountants and talking-point script-writers. For him the fun must be in the performative side of things, polishing your Italia Conti ability to magic up a fact-free world just by the use of fancy language and a compelling beard, and getting right up into the big boys' team in the culture wars big tent.

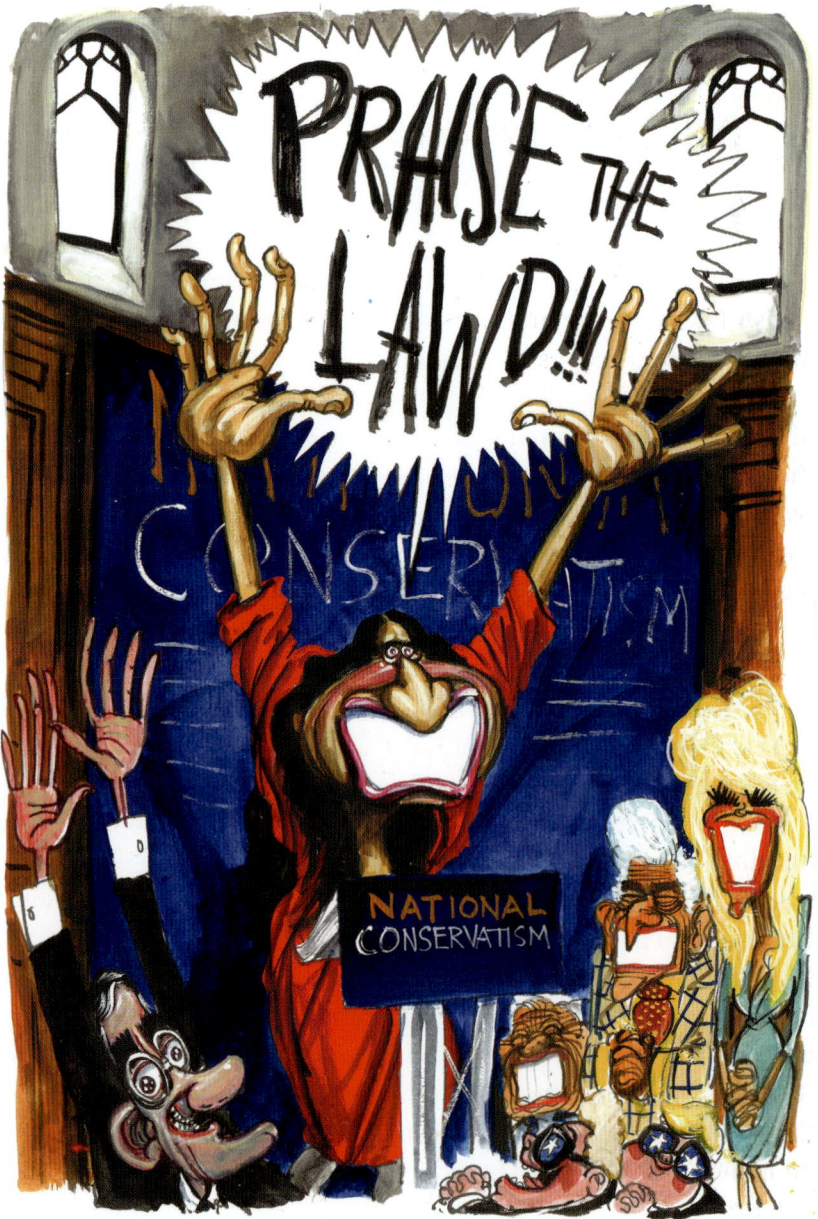

7 NatCon: Family, Flag and Faith

I wish I'd known about the National Conservatism Conference in May 2023.[98] I'd have signed up like a shot. I know the place: the Emmanuel Centre in Westminster. I've been to lots of talking shops of the Intelligence Squared 'debate and panel discussion' variety there.[99] *And I could walk there from home.* It's a rather good late twenties sort-of church built for the Christian Scientists by Sir Herbert Baker, the Lutyens of South Africa, who built the official parts of Pretoria. The impressive entrance is built in red-brick barrel vaulting, dramatic with white marble staircases.

The National Conservatism Conference promised everything, not just the British Conservative Party but the beating heart of it, the *ism*. The Emmanuel, a conference centre since 1997, is absolutely the right venue with its *look* – a cross between a church and a better-end American public building – and its setting, at the absolute heart of political geek-land.

But I wasn't quick enough off the mark. It didn't matter, as it turned out, because absolutely *everything* from the official show (not the drinks in the side rooms of course) was online, and clever friends had snuck in too. What fascinated me was the idea of seeing ardent right-wing Brits talking about 'family, flag and faith' in the most American-international of contexts. The organisers, the Edmund Burke Foundation, are a think tank led by Yoram Hazony,[100] an Israeli–American right-wing philosopher and Judeo-nationalist. The first conferences were held between 2019 and 2020 in London,

Washington and Rome. Then in Orlando (2021), Brussels (2022), Miami (2022) and then back to London in 2023.

So though it's staged in Westminster it doesn't say London particularly, and though it's called National Conservatism it doesn't sound much like the Conservative and Unionist Party (formally renamed in 1909) either. Nor, if you look at previous speakers, who've included Florida governor Ron DeSantis, the Italian prime minister Georgia Meloni, the Silicon Valley super-investor Peter Thiel and the Hungarian prime minister Viktor Orbán, they don't look particularly British either.

The money behind the Edmund Burke Foundation in Washington hasn't been completely documented and updated. But according to Open Democracy's Peter Geoghegan, writing in June 2023, they received just under a million dollars in 2019, including $400,000 from the National Christian Foundation. There'll be a lot more than that by now. They also have money from DonorsTrust – described as a 'dark money fund', since most of its donors are anonymous.[101]

When you look at the background of previous speakers, there are what most people would have seen as quite bangingly un-English elements, the first of which is the very full-on religious strand combining (American) evangelism, hardline conservative Catholicism and Israeli ultra-Orthodoxy (Hazony is a one-time aide to Netanyahu). 'One-nation' Tories – now completely out of the Conservative power picture – tended to be polite Anglicans who thought religious ranting-on was low rent. And yesterday's free-market/libertarian types mostly didn't bother with God. The Emmanuel Centre still has a big cross in the hall and religious inscriptions in the auditorium so it's caught the new speakers' mood.

The other thing is Viktor Orbán,[102] the Eastern European odd-man-out, the one who stood out against more EU aid to Ukraine, the one who's so pally with Putin. The Hungarians have something think-tanky called the MCC based in Brussels, which had a stall at the conference. And the MCC employ Frank Furedi,[103] the former patron saint of the Revolutionary Communist Party, and now of the

Baroness Claire Fox tendency of ultra-rightists (all the same people). Their curious empire includes a number of names, including *Spiked* magazine and the Battle of Ideas. The inclusion of the Hungarians as part of the gang was an absolute no for Conservatives until very recently, which is why the previous London conference in 2020 had only one backbench Conservative MP. This time, however, there were two Cabinet members – Michael Gove and Suella Braverman – and a cluster of serving MPs who were well placed for profile-raising. It seemed as if, in just three years, the lines on the road had changed.

And as for what they said, the Americans were being very American and the Brits – who would have mocked it as banging-on until recently – were trying to catch the rhythm, *and even go one better*.

The great question was whether we little British people could really follow this kind of American–international rhetoric out of the red brick and white marble of the Emmanuel Centre into the wider world. While Brits are hugely receptive to American ideas – far more than mainland Europe – the stuff we go for tends to come from big city America, from the north-east and California, not Alabama and Arizona. Could America's old culture wars themes really make a beach head here in a new right-wing party, glued together from the Tory right, plus Reform UK (not really a membership party) and who knows what else after the next election? What was clear, however, is that this initially strange foreign-seeming group had somehow become a fixture in Tory-land, bearing out Matthew d'Ancona's crucial analysis 'Bannon's Britain' (2019) in Tortoise,[104] in which he charted the 21st-century New World connections between right-wing Westminster and their Washington counterparts. It's interesting to follow the highest profile British right-wingers in the political and media worlds and see who they're talking to and where in the world they are (Nigel Farage's biographer, Michael Crick,[105] told me recently he reckoned Farage was in America about once a month now).

In America, prominent right-wing Brits get money and support and they learn about the 'political technologies' that underwrite culture wars as a practice and a profession. They get into the rhythms of political rhetoric they once might –particularly the Oxbridge ones – have found more than a bit naff and overblown. In the US context, it'd have sounded different. And as their new advisors will have told them, *it really works.*

Let's take Danny Kruger, David Cameron's speechwriter from 2006 and Boris Johnson's political secretary in 2019. He's the son of national treasure Prue Leith, Notting Hill restauranteur, late-blooming TV star, etc. etc. He's Eton and Oxford, MP for Devizes. He's hardly red wall. And yet he said the following, about "the weird medley of transgressive ideas that is now threatening the basis of civilization in the West. We have overseen the radicalization of a generation in the name of a new ideology, a new religion – a mix of Marxism and narcissism and paganism, self-worship and nature worship all wrapped up in revolution."

Now, roll that round on your tongue, dear reader. What *is* he getting at? Do you know *anyone* who signed up to this curious mixture of ideas he's suggesting? They're talking points you couldn't have identified last week, either as a subscriber or an accuser. Did you ever hear people in 2022 muttering darkly about paganism, nature worship and revolution on your daily round? Nor me!

Mr Kruger's friend and collaborator, Miriam Cates,[106] the Tory MP for Penistone and Stocksbridge in South Yorkshire, was clear on what Britain needed: effectively, *more native fertility*. Britain's men/women/couples/young people – however you frame it – were giving up on the sacred purpose of their unions. It was a public purpose – and we all know it – to make more British babies for British people. The dark forces that opposed baby-making – the selfish and downright unpatriotic forces – were on the left. This is what she actually said:

> There is one critical outcome that liberal individualism has completely failed to deliver and that is babies.
>
> Wanting to reproduce is – biologically – the most natural desire

in the world. And having children is a sign of hope for the future, of believing that your family, community and nation are good places to bring up a child.

She also said:

Having a home, a secure job and support from your family, community and nation are not the only pre-conditions to starting a family. You must also have hope for the future.

And that hope is sadly diminishing in so many of our young people today.

Because liberal individualism has proven to be completely powerless to resist the cultural Marxism that is systematically destroying our children's souls.

When culture, schools and universities openly teach that:

- our country is racist
- our heroes are villains
- humanity is killing the earth
- you are what you desire
- diversity is theology
- boundaries are tyranny and
- self-restraint is oppression.

Is it any wonder that mental health conditions, self-harm, suicide and epidemic levels of anxiety characterise the emerging generation?[107]

There we go with cultural Marxism again. Attributing all sorts of current ideas and raging rhetorics that hadn't been invented back then to a group of Jewish leftie philosophers who met up in Frankfurt in 1923. Ms Cates and Mr Kruger share something central to the National Conservatism spirit: their shared evangelical convictions.[108] [109] Evangelicalism – though declining through the age cohorts, even in the US – nonetheless remains hugely important in American politics. Over the last 30-plus years of massively funded right-wing fightback, evangelicals have been pulled into the fight, according to Anne Nelson, the author of *Shadow Network: Media, Money and the Secret Hub of the Radical Right*, which describes the workings of the American right's high command, led by the shadowy Council for National Policy.

The mood in modern rightism revealed at the Conference now hinges on the crucial idea of being 'post-liberal'. The old centre-right Conservatives and Republicans both got a constant drubbing at NatCon for being *globalist and neoliberals* – any hate-word you can throw at the 80s Thatcher and Reagan alliance while still supposedly revering Thatcher and Reagan themselves. The charge is that they let down the left-behinds, hollowed out the manufacturing base, and let cheap Chinese goods in everywhere. The City and Wall Street amoral 'elites' are central to this story, which implicitly – they're careful how exactly they say it – puts a fair few of the Tory Cabinet/shadow Cabinet members from the 1990s onwards straight into the firing line. The other part of 'post-liberal' is *social liberalism* (remember that for Americans 'liberal' means practically communist!). 'Crazed' progressive ideas – feminism, the 'gay agenda', multiculturalism, Black Lives Matter, trans rights and eco-zealots are all to blame!

We heard constantly that those changes, those movements, the whole nine yards from the 60s on, have ruined America and were ruining us too. Suella Braverman, then home secretary, was an important speaker (allegedly the only one who used autocue!). Suella Braverman loves American-born cliches bought by the yard, like sounding-off about 'tofu-eating wokerati' in 'North London townhouses', and she employed them to dramatise her fight against the supposedly invading hordes of asylum-seeking boat people. She didn't disappoint. Her best bits came when she was presenting herself – the daughter of immigrants – as the leading defender of our borders. So she said:

> I'm not embarrassed to say that I love Britain. No true conservative is. It's not racist for anyone, ethnic minority or otherwise, to want to control our borders.
>
> I reject the left's argument that it is hypocritical for someone from an ethnic minority to know these facts; to speak these truths.

My parents came here through legal and controlled migration. They spoke the language. They threw themselves into the community, embraced British values.

When they arrived they signed up to be part of our shared project because the UK meant something to them. Integration was part of the quid pro quo.[110]

The overstated nationalism is different from understated English patriotism as Orwell explained in 1945[111] and the god delusion factor meant that, while for NatCon it made good copy, no one was quite sure what it really meant here, apart from jostling for post-election positions. In fact, it was a positive *festival of new culture wars themes for 2024 and the key word, the crucial theme, was 'national'.* 'National' sweeps up everything from boat people to footballers taking the knee to offshoring jobs and on to the rather John Buchan-esque idea of *the enemy within.* The Tory Cabinet couldn't possibly say that collectively, but if you were jostling for position you could. And if you were already working as a think-tanker or an 'influencer' for an American 'shadow network' entity, you certainly could. Richard Tice,[112] the leader of Reform (formally a business rather than a membership party),[113] the third generation of a rich family construction and development company, could reasonably put his organisation's slogan on the platform as 'Make Britain Great', confident in the knowledge that his will-he-won't-he Reform colleague Nigel Farage had spent quality time at Trump rallies as the opening act.

In April 2024, NatCon became a big story in the UK. Its latest National Conservatism Conference, scheduled for Brussels on 16–17 April 2024 and part sponsored by the Brussels-based Hungarian-owned think tank MCC, run by Frank Furedi, former Emeritus Professor of Sociology at Kent University (and mentor of the Claire Fox tendency), was almost left homeless after its original venue, the Concert Noble, decided to pull out after public pressure and even threats of public protests. The conference – starring a Europe-wide cast of right-wing nationalists – was set to host Nigel Farage, Suella

Braverman – and most controversial of all – the Hungarian prime minister, Viktor Orbán. At the last minute the Sofitel Brussels seemed to have saved them. And then there was a move to another venue. There was nothing of this overheated kind in Westminster.

In the third venue, Claridge, things really hotted up and made the big UK news bulletins at last. The local left-wing mayor banned the event, in a rather high-handed way, and sent in the police. This meant big drama with Nigel Farage, one of the earlier speakers who had his say before it became chaotic, being interviewed everywhere saying this was the suppression of free speech and the excuses for it were "cobblers". A spokesperson for Rishi Sunak appeared to support the conference in a late statement.[114] All in all, as some wags said, "you couldn't buy publicity like that". Another way of putting it would be that otherwise the idea of British politicians – including one who'd recently been home secretary – sharing the stage with a kind of pan-European cast list might've passed almost unremarked by most 'mainstream' media.

Ultra Low
emission

ULEZ

ZONE

At all times

TOFU

TOFU

8 Uxbridge

Uxbridge is a hard one. Is it London or not? People from the big central London boroughs would say not. Is it representative of a group of boroughs just outside, in the way that rich and desirable Richmond leads a flotilla including Kew, Twickenham and other pleasant places? Not really. The link many Londoners might make is between the Uxbridge Road (which does carry on all the way out) and Notting Hill Gate roundabout – centre of smart London – where it starts. The other very known thing about Uxbridge is that it was recently *Boris Johnson's constituency* until a by-election, along with two other constituencies far out of London, on Thursday 20 July 2023.

In his campaigning, however, Steve Tuckwell, the Tory candidate chosen to replace Boris for Uxbridge and South Ruislip, *practically never mentioned his predecessor*. Instead, he talked constantly about an evil new invention, which the metropolitan elite were shortly to foist on Uxbridge (the met elite, for his purposes, included his Labour competitor Danny Beales, *who lived in Camden*). But his villain of the day was London mayor Sadiq Khan, the imposer of ULEZ (ironically Khan hadn't been the original ULEZ advocate – *that had been Boris Johnson*. Kahn merely inherited and ran with it). But ULEZ, in Steve Tuckwell's telling, was a 'luxury belief' pushed by those ultimate luxury believers... *environmentalists*.

According to the Tories, ULEZ was part of the double whammy that threatened Uxbridge's poorer residents; it meant people with older, non-compliant cars would immediately have to buy newer ones they couldn't afford. The other half was that they – the 'eco-zealots', the woke mob, whoever – would turn up at your door any minute and rip out your gas central heating boiler and demand you stump up for a very expensive heat pump.

The two other constituencies with by-elections that day were Somerton and Frome in Somerset and Selby and Ainsty in North Yorkshire. Both overturned huge Tory majorities in favour of Labour and the Lib Dems respectively. The Labour win was spectacular – the biggest since 1997.[115] But the Conservatives just scraped back in Uxbridge, where the smart money was mainly on another Labour win.

The post-mortems settled on a *local* factor whose priority outdid the *national* issues, where Labour was already miles ahead. *It was all down to ULEZ, which gave Rishi Sunak and his campaign organisers the idea that culture wars about the climate crisis might just help save the Tories.* They'd been weaponising climate change in the US for years which meant the off-the-shelf experience and rhetoric was available from their many friends in Washington. Isaac Levido, an American-trained Australian, by then the Tories campaign manager, knew them all by heart; he'd run his mentor Sir Lynton Crosby's Washington office.

The 21st-century culture war playbook against environmentalists doesn't start with climate change denial now. Instead, it targets the people themselves. It says *they're not your kind*, they're *eco-zealots*, who think so big and long term that they don't care what happens to ordinary people in the here and now. They're *privileged*; they all come from 'the elite' (does that sound like your Just Stop Oil protesting daughter, dear reader?). They've never had to worry about jobs and money like you and me. And they talk, in an irritating fancy way, as if everyone could afford to make those trade-offs (and don't get me started on their intentionally terrible clothes).

The second key point for culture warriors – they make it about their opponents all the time – is that these hypocritical people are *immensely powerful.* Amazingly, they've got all the institutions and the media under their control. And they want you under their control too, so they can dictate to you, stop you doing things for your family and make you follow the woke rules for life – just like the Covid lockdown supporters.

Rishi went into action within days, stopping the enforced scrappage schemes for older cars. And giving interviews everywhere saying he was *on the side of the motorist*, the martyr of the moment. And for the family, when it came time to scrap the boiler. Never mind the fact that newer cars and boilers are far cheaper to run and maintain. On 31 July 2023, Sunak announced a raft of licences for new UK fossil fuel explorations in the North Sea – 100 of them to be precise. Drill, baby, drill. They said it made sense because, since Ukraine, *energy security was a national priority.*

A series of speeches followed, in which the PM rowed back on net zero. Not on the commitment to it *in principle*, because no one trying to give the impression that he had restored order after Johnson and Truss could say that and hold on to the Tory blue wall. Instead, in an act of magical thinking, he said we in the UK were such climate pioneers that we could give ourselves a break and take a bit longer now and spare not just the motorist martyrs he'd adopted, but everyone struggling to make ends meet. Which people took to mean that things would go on as usual because it would magically come out all right if you *don't look now.* Parliamentary sketch writers had a field day with the country's richest MP Rishi Sunak, a constant hirer of private planes, talking about everyday economics. Sunak's media supporters turned up the heat on environmentalists with their characterisation of them as eco-zealots, a sort of crazed sect who loved gluing themselves to things and stopping ambulances getting to emergencies.

Just Stop Oil, founded in 2022, first appeared as major protestors in April 2022 and were constantly on SMET front pages. They'd had a fair bit of practice for it with Extinction Rebellion and particularly with Greta Thunberg, working out how best to hatchet her without sounding like misogynistic child abusers (the answer was broadly a) we blame the parents, b) obviously autistic, poor thing! and c) foreign, they're not like us, what's she doing here?).

Even the SMET papers knew better by then than to flatly deny global warming, or even challenge its likely schedule. The move from 'experts' – academics, Al Gore and the rest – to noisy-often-young-protestors gave the tabloids exactly what they needed to attack.

The *Mail* employed its favourite tactic against Just Stop Oil. On 17 February 2024, a box in a story on the group featured 'The posh background of Just Stop Oil's poster girl', Phoebe Plummer. Phoebe had been raised in a £4 million house near the King's Road in Chelsea. She'd been at £45,000 a year St Mary's Ascot, then at the £34,000 a year Mander Portman Woodward College in Kensington, thence to Manchester University for computer science ending up reading Social Anthropology at SOAS in London. Got the picture? Apparently pink-haired Phoebe has already been arrested for a string of disturbances. After that you'd know not to be involved in Just Stop Oil, wouldn't you? Not your sort of person...

On 19 January 2023, 'Deny, Deceive, Delay', the second of two reports from the Institute for Strategic Dialogue (ISD) set out their findings from research into 'New Trends in Climate Mis- and Disinformation at COP27'.[116] The first report had identified some of the themes and actions involved in globally coordinated campaigns against climate change actions of all kinds.

The report recognised a growing theme of culture wars initiatives towards an us-and-them approach. Newer agendas that appeared at COP27 were swiftly worked into anti-woke and conspiracist movements. Rather than just sharing stories about, say, the dubious emission claims made against electric vehicles, or the uselessness of climate change action in the West while China and India remained as massive polluters, the story became one of the woke eco-zealots forcing climate action on ordinary people. The woke eco-zealots were, of course, the same (metropolitan) 'liberal elites' who were doing everything else. They were behind strange indoctrination in schools, attacks on our heritage (statues, etc.), trans rights and identity politics generally. Just the woke mob again!

At the same time, the ISD report remarked on "a stark comeback for climate change denial, reminiscent of arguments from the 1970s". They also noted negligence from Big Tech companies who had signed up to act against disinformation. The fact is that exciting, contentious disinformation makes money for social media operators because, as the earlier report had explained, it had faster, wider circulation than any authoritative fact-checked material. An online lie was *always* halfway around the world before the truth had got its boots on. After the pandemic and the Ukraine invasion, the ISD noted a new emphasis on "livelihoods, national security and sovereignty". 'Energy independence', for instance, turned up verbatim in 1,925 mentions in Meta's Ad Library then.[117]

Following climate lies around the world and identifying the organisers and pundits who push them on is grimly fascinating. There's a mass of stories and angles, from a wide range of posters, but some so persistent and at such a scale they were clearly bots, and some of them clearly 'state actors' like Russia or China. Some of the themes seemed contradictory – gung-ho posts saying that we absolutely needed more oil and gas now, while others said the fossil fuel industry was doing everything that was needed. It didn't matter; this wasn't a university debate, and the different stories would all find their mark. The online culture wars context allowed new contributors to the arguments, people who loved getting in there for the hell of it, not because they had skin in the game, and not because they were paid lobbyists, but because they wanted to attack and – in the classic culture wars phrase – 'own the libs'. It could be fun. It was all just a game to them.

Some familiar UK faces showed up in this pile-on, so Brendan O'Neill, political editor of the *Spiked* site (part of the curious cohort of former Revolutionary Communist Party turned right-wing populist organisations spearheaded by Claire Fox – Baroness Fox of Buckley – and their inspirational guru Frank Furedi), said in the *Daily Mail*: "I was a Sunak sceptic. But taking on culture warriors, eco-zealots and sex offenders has proved he DOES have political fire in his belly."[118] "A result for Rishi!" is what O'Neill said on 26 September 2023.

He'd already said in *Spiked* that "eco-dread is a luxury belief we can no longer afford". He goes on to say that climate change actions are "the fantasies of a global elite". Them again! But who exactly are they? I think we should be told![119]

Right-wing populist attacks involve favourite names that come up everywhere in relation to practically everything. The dimmest callers to James O'Brien's phone-in show on LBC radio like to display their secret knowledge of any conspiracy they've bought into by identifying Bill Gates and George Soros as the founders and funders (more on them shortly). Both are ineffably rich and undeniably influential in having stepped out of line, relatively late in life, to do relatively active philanthropic things. Gates is particularly seen as part of the Big Pharma plot, forcing people across the world to take the Covid jab because:

(a) he profited from jabs as an investor (false);

(b) the vaccines contained super-small microchips which would surveil everyone and help his world domination campaign (also, shockingly, false).[120]

And hedge-funder Soros was behind every woke grouping you could think of everywhere. Open Democracy, which Soros supports in the UK, had a secret role in organising every kind of activism going. These people must be Suella Braverman's "tofu-eating wokerati". Where are they? Apparently they're in "North London town houses" so they could just be in my old manor! If they're in North London and eat funny food, they could so easily fall into another important populist category: the cultural Marxists again. Well, you would, wouldn't you? How exactly those ancient secret commies aligned with the super-rich global elites – the private plane hypocrites of every climate change conference – didn't matter. Nothing had to make sense, *it was the feeling that counted.*

What did matter was that the new anti-environmentalist super-spreaders were culture war celebrities like the Canadian psychologist Jordan Peterson, who had moved from his original

Baden-Powellish *12 Rules for Life* to talking up every populist right-wing argument going (he spent quality time online endorsing Helen Joyce's book *Trans*, which blamed the 'trans-activist' lobby for practically everything else going).

Relative calm has been restored to verdant Uxbridge in 2024. Mr Tuckwell, the new Tory MP, made his maiden speech in Parliament on 13 November 2023, explaining just what a lovely place it is – "vibrant" was the word he used. ULEZ was rolled out to all London boroughs on 29 August 2023. But on 1 October 2023, the *Independent* reported "one month after Ulez expanded, Uxbridge residents are still angry".[121] Vigilantes have attacked ULEZ cameras. The police recorded 510 crimes related to them up to 31 August 2023. And in a soothing gesture, Mayor Sadiq Khan announced an increase in the scrappage payment for vans.

BEFORE   AFTER

9 Race Wars

We're all bound to be replaced, but some of us fear it more acutely than others. Large-scale research at Cambridge University (funded by the Leverhulme Trust) looking at the uptake of conspiracy theories in the Western world identified one that was widely believed across a range of countries, including the UK.[122]

It's the Great Replacement theory[123] whose supporters believe there is an ongoing plot to replace all the white people in the UK with Muslims and to introduce sharia law in place of our current rules. In the more detailed expositions of the theory, this process is described as being directed by a shadowy group of 'globalist', elite types, which is generally assumed to mean what used to be called 'rootless cosmo-politans'.

Whenever you come across this sort of reference it often means the Jewish Hungarian-born billionaire hedge-funder George Soros, who is clearly stupendously energetic even in his 90s. Or it might just be Bill Gates, the philanthropic Microsoft billionaire (worth US$127.4bn)[124] *plus* George Soros. Or some combo of the kind. People who support right-wing conspiracy theories very often attribute bad things to those two.

They're neither of them angels, but how exactly could they get around to all of it? And why should either or both of them want to organise Muslim takeovers? The original idea comes from a French white supremacist author called Renaud Camus (not to be confused with that other French writer Albert Camus, who was an undeniable leftie) in his 2011 book *Le Grand Remplacement*. It spread very rapidly across Europe among ultra-rightists – there were a fair few there already – and then to America. Unsurprisingly its most convinced and proactive proselytisers have come from Steve Bannon-land but this is differentially acknowledged by the foot soldiers of the theory. The idea of the organiser being globalist – the international liberal elite of some kind – is enough to be going along with for most believers.

Anyway, the Cambridge study – carried out over many years with large samples and all the indicators of reliability by CRASSH (Centre for Research in the Arts, Social Sciences and Humanities) – showed in 2018 that 31% of UK respondents who voted Leave believed in the GRT, but only 6% of Remainers did.[125] It's a massive difference. If nearly a third of the Leave voters believed they and theirs were somehow up for the chop and also believed that EU-style globalists were somehow at the heart of the plot, some people might just argue that it could have had some influence on their choices in the 2016 referendum, which was a close-run thing. And if you'd thought that Turkey was joining the EU imminently – a story pushed by the Leave comms people – giving all roughly 85 million Turks immediate and untrammelled legal entrée to everywhere in the UK from Tonbridge to Totnes and you didn't like the sound of that either, it could also have played on your mind.

When listeners call the battling centrist LBC phone-in host James O'Brien about the 2016 referendum's outcome, as they still do, they tend to cite the 'take back control' line and that lovely long plangent word 'sovereignty' as describing what they wanted. It almost always turns out that they couldn't say how the EU's rules had restricted their own lives, but they weren't keen on foreigners invading the country and taking over. When asked, they tended to wildly overstate the numbers of immigrants in the UK, particularly Muslims. An Ipsos review found the public thinks that *around 1 in 6 Britons* are Muslim (in fact there are about 1 in 16 or 6.3% of the UK population.)[126]

The notion of Muslims *taking over* because all the UK elites were too scared, or too PC/woke to do anything about it – or were *actually in league* with the takers-over – surged back onto the top of the culture wars hit list in early 2024 because of the Israel/Gaza war and the ceasefire protests. And Lee Anderson MP. What could we do without Lee Anderson, until recently the Tory party's token working-class person? Lee Anderson said on GB News on 22 February 2024 that *the Islamists had taken over London* by taking over its mayor Sadiq Khan, who is a Muslim. This meant that what some people had called the "pro-Palestinian hate mob" – meaning the ceasefire protest marchers – had, so Lee implied, been softly policed. Rishi Sunak sacked him – he obviously had to – but couldn't/wouldn't explain why; it was just "wrong" he said (and so did his Cabinet colleagues in every crazed interview that followed). But people TV vox-popped in Anderson's constituency of Ashfield weren't so sure. It was 'free speech' after all.

The Cambridge research found that the British concern about immigrants taking over was significantly matched in America. A full 42% of Trump voters from 2016 were Great Replacement believers, while a mere 3% of Clinton voters believed it. But who exactly did they think was going to do all this US replacement?

The Muslim population in the US wasn't that well placed for the job – there are 3.45 million Muslims in the US, meaning just over 1% of a population of 331.9 million. If, as a shadowy global elitist type, you were trying to engineer a Muslim takeover of the US from a base of just over 1% of the population, you couldn't get that far, however energetically they reproduced. So perhaps they had Mexicans in mind, or the total of non-white Americans of all kinds.

Many Americans believe in the same theory as UK Leavers do, but in a different situation, with a slightly different mix of culprits – a combination of the Democratic party trying to create a more pro-Dem electorate, plus the usual so-called Jewish globalists. In 2022 Washington website 'The Hill' reported that 61% of Trump 2020 voters believed in the Great Replacement theory, and 16% of Biden voters endorsed it in a Yahoo News YouGov poll that May.[127] It sounded like a very significant uptick. The Cambridge analysis hasn't been updated but what's the betting the GRT buy-in has grown in the UK too?

Like most conspiracy theories at this scale, it doesn't make any sense at all, but it doesn't need to. *Culture war messages reach the parts other messages can't reach.* The anxieties people can't explain or acknowledge. The anxieties about status and security – about your place in the world and your tribe's place in the world. That's why a toxic kind of class anxiety now makes some version of the race and immigration story the front line of the culture wars across the West, and that's why Lee Anderson MP waded in as he did. He's got form here; according to former Conservative MP Anna Soubry he was expelled from the Labour Party for racism.[128] And his attack on Sadiq Khan was simply fulfilling his epic promise to plunge into the culture wars as a first shot in Tory electioneering, but he'll be speaking for the Reform party next time. The Conservatives have let him find his own level now, but there's the danger of further defection to Reform to manage. In the meantime, the Tories can leave the story to spread on the new right-wing platforms on the assumption that it can help them when the election comes. This is why all the right-wing press has described the Gaza ceasefire protests as if they were raging ISIS rallies.

In a widely communicated combination of No. 10 meetings and a speech at the Community Security Trust (CST, a charity which fights antisemitism) annual dinner on 28 February 2024, PM Rishi Sunak said we were in danger of "mob rule". What he meant was the scale and number of the pro-Palestinian ceasefire protests, the protests outside Tory MP Tobias Ellwood's house and a projection of a pro-Palestine image onto Big Ben all jammed together. All completely *attributable* events, but carefully not described as 'Islamist'. Sunak left the viewers to form their own conclusions. The right-wing press (85%-plus of newspaper sales)[129] obediently endorsed the Sunak line the following morning. "Sunak tells police chiefs it's time to end 'mob rule'," said the *Daily Mail*, the UK's biggest-selling title.

British newspapers have form on these issues. In a report prepared for the United Nations High Commission for Refugees (probably not your average Conservative's favourite organisation), in 2015 Mike Berry, Inaki Garcia-Blanco and Kerry Moore looked at press coverage of the refugee and migrant crises in the EU; a content analysis of five European countries.[130] The analysts concluded that the UK was off the scale in its hostility: "among those countries surveyed, Britain's right-wing media was uniquely aggressive in its campaigns against refugees and migrants. What distinguished the right-of-centre press in the UK was the degree to which that section of the press campaigned aggressively against refugees and migrants". (Interestingly a Europe-wide study of newspaper readers conducted by Pew in 2018 showed that British national newspapers were the least trusted in their home country of those in the national situations surveyed.)

The class dimension is absolutely central to immigration's role in the culture wars. In Western countries, with an increasing divide between the status and prospects of graduates and non-graduates, educated people are forever remarking between themselves – they know not to say it publicly now – that the crucial divide on so many of the culture wars issues is education (the figures show it).[131] Non-graduates overwhelmingly favoured Trump in the USA[132] and more educated Democrats sometimes assume privately they can't think the issues through logically – that they're economic turkeys voting for Christmas. But Trump's voters feel they now know perfectly well where they stand in a changing world and what really matters to them, and it's more than money. They want respect and they feel they're not getting it. That's why Trump said he liked "poorly educated" people at his 2016 Nevada Republican presidential caucuses, which went to the heart of it.[133] Apparently, clever educated people don't seem to understand the raging status anxiety of people who see themselves as losing even what little they've got! It's the relativities that matter.

In a decade of rising inequalities and declining living standards in 'middle America', scapegoats simplify and energise a depressing situation. *It helps to have someone to hate.* If lucky liberals don't understand your problems you know someone who will, someone who won't call you stupid or a racist. Culture wars have gone – as James Davison Hunter, the American author of the original 1991 book on them acknowledges – from being a debate between relatively small groups of educated people to the focus of national political polarisation. Graduate numbers have spiralled and the internet lets everyone in on a shouting match without the legacy media gatekeepers. In the USA, so Hunter says, culture wars have taken over politics.[134]

The race divide works differently here. We've got a different inheritance, and a different media ecology, though even that is under attack from new explicitly political platforms like GB News. We tell ourselves constantly that we're better, more comfortable about race than most European countries, and certainly than the US. And it's partly true. But we can never get complacent. The Great Replacement theory has proved horribly inspirational to mass murderers across the world. The manifestos of shooters like the Norwegian Anders Breivik (he killed 77 young people in Oslo and Utøya), the Christchurch shooter Brenton Tarrant (who killed 50 Muslims in New Zealand) and the 18-year-old Buffalo shooter Payton S. Gendron (he killed 10 black Americans on 14 May 2022 in Buffalo) all cited the Great Replacement theory or white genocide as their inspiration. At the white supremacist rally at Charlottesville, Virginia on 12 August 2017, some of the protestors carried Swastika placards and chanted "Jews will not replace us". They've been emboldened even further by Donald Trump's comment afterward, in August 2017, that "you had people that were very fine people, on both sides".[135]

The immigrant culture war has been revived as a key strand in the febrile mix of Conservative campaigning and the jockeying for power on the right. What will the new UK right-wing party configuration at the end of 2024 after the world's most successful political party falls apart?[136] It's seen as a combination of some right-wing Tories with figures and groupings formerly on the margins and immigration as a central policy issue, from the Reform UK party on. Or, in other words, the right-wing configurations of Steve Bannon's Britain. Something more like the European far-right parties that Bannon has ostentatiously fostered and linked, from Marine Le Pen's National Rally in France to Viktor Orbán's Fidesz in Hungary.

We saw Bannon on British TV screens in February 2024 at the

Conservative Political Action Conference (CPAC) in Maryland. He was on a panel with Liz Truss and described the British far-right figure "Tommy Robinson' as "a hero". Liz Truss, the UK's shortest-serving prime minister in history appeared to agree, saying "that is correct". Tommy Robinson, whose anti-Muslim activities were mainly supported by rich right-wing Americans, was serving a 13-month prison sentence four years ago when Bannon called him "the backbone of the UK". But, as Peter Jukes pointed out in *Byline Times*, "this is the first time such a senior Conservative has endorsed him". Bannon himself was a potential jailbird, investigated and indicted for fraudulently using funds raised for his 'Build the Wall' US–Mexico barrier project in 2020. Outgoing president Donald Trump granted him a last-minute pardon for his federal offences in 2021 but, as Jukes points out, he still faces "state-level" charges in New York later this year.

Bannon has used race and immigration unambiguously as a culture war issue and famously encouraged others in his network of European rightists. In 2018 he told an audience at the party congress of France's far-right National Rally in the French city of Lille, "Let them call you racist. Let them call you xenophobes. Let them call you nativists. Wear it as a badge of honor. Because every day, we get stronger and they get weaker."

Nearer home, Bannon became very matey with Boris Johnson when he was foreign secretary in Theresa May's government back in 2016 to 2018. In an American documentary Bannon told the story of co-writing Johnson's resignation speech in London in July 2018. Johnson fiercely denies this, while Bannon merely smiles. Soon after in widely quoted articles credited to Bannon's influence, Johnson famously described Muslim women in London as looking like "bank robbers" and "letterboxes". He'd been more careful before, with his 'one nation' pretentions on various soft social issues.[137] But this time, it looked as if he'd been taken up into Trump-World. On 19 January 2024 Johnson confirmed this by announcing, in the *Daily Mail*, that he was backing Trump in the American election.[138]

10 Freedom Riders

Are you in favour of freedom? Freedom from – well, practically everything? Are you what Americans call a libertarian? It's all the rage there, I can tell you. Freedom to bear arms, to have your own little all-American stash of AR-15 rifles. Freedom from government trying to boss you about and make you pay taxes and denying you your right to pollute or to pay your workers whatever you want. Freedom from regulation – which is what *socialists* do, regulate everything in sight.

Above all, are you in favour of freedom of speech? Your right to say what other people might allege is a bit on the nasty side. Even when it's what some might call *hate speech*? Do you say constantly "I may disapprove of what you say, but I will defend to the death your right to say it"?[139] It's a big thing, a big gambit now in right-wing culture wars territory, freedom of speech – claiming to give a voice to the voiceless and downtrodden who Must Not Be Silenced. The big idea is that The Institutions – universities, media, law, etc. – are the bogeymen because they've all been taken over by the woke mob now and must be held well back to protect the little, medium-sized or even very big man or woman.

Quite a lot of current American freedom of speech talk really comes down to the rights of those very big types. It derives from nineteenth-century reactions to revolutions – particularly the French and American ones – and the 1848 mood.[140] Powerful people, initially aristocrats – and then mostly plutocrats – didn't want to be constrained by increasingly democratic governments, emerging trade unions and the rest. But convenient thinkers arrived with a whole re-conception of freedom as *individual rights*, rather than collective ones, and a flood of plangent position papers followed. Out of all this developed a whole new 20th-century profession of clever communicators who worked for those big people – the ones who could afford to pay them (the convenient thinkers increasingly *said* they supported the little men, but the big ones actually paid the bills). "A man's right to work as he will to spend what he earns to own property, to have the State as servant and not as master, these are the British inheritance," as Margaret Thatcher said in 1975 in what was called her 'rich men have rights' speech.[141]

They gave the big men a new voice and out of this came, for instance, the invention of 'front groups' – they're called astroturf organisations now – between the wars. Organisations that pretended to be spontaneous and 'grassroots' but weren't. They were wholly invented by lobbyists/PRs from smart offices in New York and Washington, DC (London got in on the act later). These front outfits were cast and scripted to do what the client needed, to give their arguments a voice, but one coming from convincing *relatable* grassroots citizen types.

These front organisations had vague, high-minded and incontrovertible names like the Women's League Against Unpleasantness or Freedom for Alabama Residents. Who could complain about that? The great pioneer of this sort of thing was Edward Bernays, the American public relations titan. Bernays was Sigmund Freud's nephew, he lived to 103 and was the inventor of a raft of front groups for commercial and government clients, including the CIA in the US.

The PR/lobbyist descendants of Bernays' discipline tend to be very keen on 'freedom' in this American sense of platforming 'difficult' organisations and individuals with difficult things to say – often so difficult that somebody else has to say them in positive ways. It's called 'third-party endorsement'. This was completely different from the 'old' collective kind of freedom – the emancipatory kind that gives people universal suffrage, the right to join a union, free healthcare or equal rights for minorities – black, gay, etc. The kinds of freedom behind successive genuinely popular reforms throughout the 20th century, and particularly after the Second World War in Britain.

The Attlee Labour government of 1945 came in with an electoral landslide of a 145-seat majority against Churchill, the Conservative war hero PM, because a battered nation wanted change. That change was set out in the Labour Party's manifesto 'Let Us Face the Future', written by its 30-year-old research director and secretary of the Policy Committee, Michael Young,[142] later Lord Young of Dartington. In a long and astonishingly innovative career, Young founded the Consumers' Association, the Open University, the Institute for Community Studies and many other useful organisations, and wrote more than 30 books,[143] the best-known of which is his dystopian satire *The Rise of the Meritocracy*.

Toby Young, the now extremely Conservative contrarian, journalist, author and media-land figure, is Michael Young's son. In Tim Fountain's one-man play about Young, *How To Lose Friends and Alienate People*, first performed in 2003 at the Soho Theatre,[144] the action starts with Toby Young in LA taking the call that may just get him in to the *Vanity Fair* Oscars afterparty in LA. He gets in by impersonating another British journalist, is hilariously rude to a variety of A-listers and then gets thrown out. That was the Toby Young people knew then: attention seeking, celebrity obsessed, constantly pranking and failing (you're excused a lot if you're funny and well connected) well into his forties.

Now, however, Young is deeply into politics and he's in the freedom business, *both in the American way*. He is the inventor and frontman of the Free Speech Union (started in February 2020). He was a speaker at 2023's American–Israeli organised National Conservatism Conference – and on a mass of right-wing platforms where he denounces woke amusingly as "Wokus Dei".

Under both hats he's a committed professional culture warrior now, and the Free Speech Union is there to save the victims of the woke persecution. It's not clear to what extent it supports anyone else. The woke mob, according to Toby, are the great leaders in persecution. He says he's there for the people who might otherwise be silenced or even sacked. Martyrs of modern cancellation. He doesn't say much about this government's cancelling of its critics or national newspapers which regularly ignore inconvenient stories, or American book-banning in schools in Republican states.[145] It's the woke he's worried about.

"Free Speech has never been at greater peril than at any time since the Second World War," says the FSU's excitable website.[146] A social media pile-on against someone who's said something out of turn can ruin lives, so they say. But the FSU, with its helpers and legal teams, are there for them. They have a Writers' Advisory Council which includes the pseudonymous thriller writer Alex Marwood, the constantly cross *Spectator* columnist Lionel Shriver (author of *We Need to Talk About Kevin*), Andrew Doyle, the rightist comedian (they're quite rare) and GB News presenter, as well as Helen Joyce, the talkative anti-trans author of *Trans*, now a campaigner for Sex Matters.

The FSU's massive overall Advisory Council – there are 46 names on it – includes Douglas Murray, one of the Anglosphere's most ubiquitous right-wing talkers; Claire Fox, now a peer and one-time organiser of the ex-Revolutionary Communist Party contingent; Julia Hartley-Brewer, looking and talking like a sort of Cruella De Vil of the Home Counties; and Professor David Starkey, in case you had any doubt where they're at. It's an absolute line-up of every raging rightist crone and drone you've ever seen. They don't seem to have bothered with even the odd token centre-leftist to suggest balance.

There are other interesting people on their Council too: the *Telegraph*'s super-angry Alison Pearson (of the *Planet Normal* podcast); the propagandist politics prof Matthew Goodwin (op. cit.); Mark Littlewood, the former director general of the IEA, now leading light of the so-called 'Popular Conservatives team' led by former PM Liz Truss; and David Goodhart, who moved from being

North London's favourite Etonian Marxist to the Centre for Policy Studies, which is another favourite Tory think tank.

But what else has the FSU actually done to help other, more modest people against censorship, cancellation and even job loss for something they said? The FSU clearly fights this fight at a rather general level, with the usual pressure group reports about proposed legislation and learned reports. But who exactly are the 2,000-plus individual cases where people's reputations and jobs have been defended since opening in 2020?

In the course of its defence of free speech, the FSU has claimed to have recruited 22,000+ members and to have aided them in well over 2,000 cases.[147]

For the most part, the FSU's public/pastoral work follows a pattern. A member has said/posted something deemed offensive at work, in person or online and has been subject to disciplinary action of some kind as a result. The FSU then, having established that if their member's rhetoric does not break freedom of expression laws or reach the threshold for a hate crime, steps in to defend the individual in the form of linking with legal aid and solicitors, sometimes financial support and general advice on proceedings.

Browsing the FSU's frequently asked questions page, you can get a sense of some of the main areas of concern where their members are likely to come into conflict with their employers. These include compliance with their company's social media policy, compelled declaration of gender pronouns, suspension of social media accounts, and unwilling participation in diversity training courses. It is on this final count that two of the FSU's most high-profile cases centre, namely the employment tribunals of Simon Isherwood and Carl Borg-Neal.

In 2021 Isherwood was dismissed by West Midlands Trains for gross misconduct following comments he made during an online diversity training session. The Free Speech Union stepped in and recruited one of the UK's leading religious rights and freedom of speech barristers, Paul Diamond, to fight Isherwood's case.

Finding in Isherwood's favour, the judge concluded that

"however contentious or odious some might regard the claimant's comments to be, the expression of his private view of the course to his wife in the confines of his own home was not blameworthy or culpable conduct". The FSU's "biggest ever legal victory"[148] came at the employment tribunal of Carl Borg-Neal, a former Lloyds bank manager who was awarded £800,000 in damages following his wrongful dismissal for comments similarly made during a diversity training session. Borg-Neal decided to pursue a compensation claim and joined the FSU, which hired solicitor Emma Hamnett at Doyle Clayton to bring the case against Lloyds. The FSU agreed to cover all his legal fees on the basis that if victorious he would repay them, which he did following their successful judgment in January 2024.

Both these incidents highlight the FSU's dislike of diversity/inclusion training in the workplace and their work surrounding language and race. Their most recent campaign regarding the banishment of FSU member Linzi Smith from Newcastle United matches highlights the organisation's now seemingly key concern: the trans debate.

Described by Toby Young as "the most egregious example of corporate interference with free speech I've ever come across" and by Helen Joyce as "one of the most sinister things I've seen in the five plus years I've been following the gross overreaches of transgender ideology",[149] Linzi Smith's case has risen since it appeared in November 2023 to the top of the FSU agenda, with their website's 'Campaigns' tab currently (June 2024) listing only this issue.

Centred around 34-year-old Newcastle United fan and 'gender-critical' lesbian Linzi Smith in 2023, the case involved Smith's three-year suspension from St James' Park following an investigation by the club and the Premier League which found her to have made a series of tweets which were deemed to be transphobic. By mid-November of that year she was informed by the club that she was banned from attending match days for the remainder of the season and for a further two years.

Through a friend, she was put in touch with Harry Miller, a former police officer who won a legal challenge against police forces recording gender-critical views as hate incidents.

He urged her to submit a subject access request to Newcastle United. When the club sent her the documentation it held on her, she found it included an 11-page dossier compiled by the Premier League, entitled 'Online Investigation and Target Profile – Linzi Smith'.

The Premier League had trawled through her social media posts to find her date of birth, where she lives and the area where she works, and discover that "they do appear to walk their dog by [XXXX] Church which is just off [the street where she lives]."[150] Smith went on to explain the offending tweets in her own words in an interview with lesbian feminist Julie Bindel.[151]

The FSU has organised a crowdfunding campaign to fund Smith's legal action against Newcastle and the Premier League, and has raised £31,509 of its £50,000 goal as I write (in July 2024). The crowdfund page notes at the very end that "any unused funds will be put towards other important gender-critical related campaigns".[152] There is good reason to believe this. In an interview with Maya Forstater (executive director of Sex Matters) at a FSU event, she let slip the revealing statistic that 40% of the cases the FSU deals with are trans based, with her pressure group regularly sending people their way.[153]

Later in the same video Eric Kaufmann, endorsing the FSU's academic and legislative work, states he is looking forward (with a knowing smirk) to the FSU "expanding abroad". In line with their UK counterparts' trans focus, Free Speech Union of Australia co-founder Dara Macdonald (formerly of the Institute for Public Affairs – 'one of the largest promoters of climate science denial in Australia' according to DeSmog)[154] stated in a recent interview that in the first three weeks of FSUA's operation (launched December 2023) all inquiries from members of the public seeking defence "apart from maybe one" were about gender pronouns[155] – topping its UK counterpart's 40% trans focus.

The FSU's best-known martyr is the actor Laurence Fox, son of posh actor James and related to the Fox family of overachieving actors. Laurence Fox for some years played Sergeant James Hathaway in ITV's *Lewis*. And he sang a bit. Some have suggested that he's not the most talented Fox family member.[156] Some even went so far as to say he only became truly famous for marrying Billie Piper (now divorced) and then becoming a non-specific political activist after a run-in with an audience member on *Question Time* in 2020 (he often talks about the cruel unfairness of the white privilege idea as applied to him).[157] And then launching his own political party, Reclaim, funded by city financier Jeremy Hosking, and standing for mayor of London in 2021.[158] Toby Young has always liked higher-end showbusiness.

At first glance it looks as if Toby has gone down a typical later-life rabbit hole of British upper-middle right-wing martyrdom by fronting the FSU. And it's a clever pitch, after all, designed to put nice thoughtful Islington centre-leftists – the kind he grew up with – in a quandary, which is what he loves doing. They're people who worry about media, about censorship leading on to authoritarianism, all that jazz. They naturally want to defend free speech even if they're wary of Toby. But look more closely at Toby Young now and it seems as if he's actually gone down something deeper and darker recently, in terms of the ideas he's espoused, the people he goes around with and those on his Advisory Council. And the very agenda-driven way things seem to work at the FSU, despite Young's breezy disingenuousness. The high-profile defence work aside, the FSU increasingly seems to work like a Westminster think tank, working far less visibly to change legislation. It's presenting ready-made ideas to government for new laws, in the hope that government will run with them.

Take the ideas, and the difficult idea of speaking up for those ideas, ideas that a majority across the electorate – not just the woke, whoever they are – would find hard going. Ideas like eugenics, a long-standing interest of Young's, which clearly pre-dates the FSU,[159] then link it to Richard Herrnstein and Charles Murray's bestselling *The Bell Curve* of 1994 – which strongly suggested a long-standing genetic link between race and intelligence and was eagerly taken up by white supremacists. Its critics systematically took Murray's thinking apart. They also pointed out that his support and data had been supplied by the Pioneer Fund,[160] an American pro-Nazi organisation set up by Wickliffe Draper in the US in 1937, when they were proselytising quite successfully in America against Jewish immigration and the expansion of the 'African–American population'. Toby Young interviewed Murray on the *Quillette* podcast (favoured platform of the 'intellectual dark web') in 2020.[161]

In 2018 Toby Young lost two roles in a row: his £90,000-a-year job for the New Schools Network (appointed in 2015) and his membership of the board at the Office for Students. He was apparently suggested for the OFS job by the then education minister Jo Johnson, brother of Boris Johnson (then foreign secretary). The appointment was allegedly a shoo-in, without much scrutiny. But then old tweets started to appear along with details of his enthusiasm and speech-making about intelligence science and eugenics.[162] He resigned from the Office for Students in January 2018 and the rest thereafter.

Young also famously suggested that "progressive eugenics" – whatever that was – might help working-class parents achieve social mobility for their children.

Provocations like seeming to espouse white supremacist-endorsed versions of intelligence science are more contentious than musing cheekily about female MPs' breasts, the kind of remark that Young had been famous for. And seeming to be one degree of separation from Peter Thiel, Steve Bannon and Viktor Orbán isn't a good look either. However you play it, it's *heavy*.

Has Toby Young actually met all these vengeful customers? It isn't clear. But the links are unavoidable. Peter Thiel's political number two, Joe Lonsdale of Palantir Technologies, was described in a *Byline* article of December 2021 as having been significantly involved in the discussions in Cambridge that led to the FSU's foundation in 2020.[163] No one's emerged to refute that, apparently. Thiel has been involved – as a speaker and a supporter – in the (very international) National Conservatism Conference – NatCon.

Toby Young was a speaker at the latest London version of NatCon in May 2023.[164]

And then another degree of separation, closer to home. Through Baroness Fox of Buckley, who's on the FSU's Advisory Council, there's the link to Viktor Orbán. The mentor to Fox (and her whole originally hard-left-moved-to-hard-right cohort) is Frank Furedi, now executive director since 2022 of MCC Brussels, the Hungarian think tank supported by Orbán's government – apparently to disrupt the EU. The Hungarian state pays Furedi's wages. Orbán, proudly a Putin pal, anti-immigration, anti-LGBTQ and the rest, is his ultimate boss.

The US hard right – Steve Bannon is a good example here – is very keen on Viktor Orbán; it holds the CPAC meetings in Hungary. And many American right-wingers go to Budapest for an Orbán pilgrimage. Orbán is very much against race mixing, like them (he's praised *The Camp of the Saints*, a French novel that inspires many new-right conspiracy theory believers who buy the Great Replacement theory).[165] He's also famously anti-trans, so he's on the line there with Bannon and friends. *They see Hungary as a model for the new America.*

Furedi, a former professor of Sociology at the University of Kent, is the acknowledged – and continuing – mentor and inspiration of one of the most extraordinary groups in British political history. They're extraordinary because they've hung together and moved together from well back in the last century until now. Over that period they've gone from an ostensibly far-left Trotskyist position as the Revolutionary Communist Party to a clearly far-right set of involvements now, particularly with the new 'nationalism' group.[166] They've gone from supporting immigration to opposing it, supporting the package of 20th-century freedoms around race and sexuality to opposing some of them – or supporting regimes that oppose them; they sometimes box clever over these things. And they are remarkable in the level of *entryism* they've achieved. A peerage from Boris Johnson for former RCP member Claire Fox. Leadership – until recently – of the No. 10 Strategy

Unit for another Furedi follower (and student), Munira Murza.

Most of the former RCP members have generated new names and initiatives at an impressive rate. The Battle of Ideas, a Claire Fox platform, launched a new initiative with the FSU in 2020. Its objective was to "invite students themselves to champion free speech and take the lead in remaking the case for critical inquiry".[167] It also gave the FSU some useful seed money – £85,574 over 2020 and 2021 according to *Byline Times*.[168]

This was the second such initiative devoted to freedom of speech and combatting wokery in UK schools and universities. 'Freedom of speech' here was code for pushing back against the woke mob (or, more conventionally, the liberal left) in its influence on political and cultural education. The first push was a far-right import from America called Turning Point UK, developed directly out of Turning Point US, a well-funded organisation that aimed to retrieve the campus from what they described as a complete left-wing takeover (again cultural Marxism was a favourite term!). One of Turning Point US's initiatives was the 'Professor Watchlist', designed to identify the leftie professors by having Turning Point students observe them and then expose them. TPUS also had its own contingent at the 6 January 2021 Capitol riot.[169]

Despite the existing links and constant platforming of young TPUK 'political commentators' on mainstream UK broadcasters, the 'Professor Watchlist', with its McCarthyist overtones, wasn't launched in the UK, and the TPUK project seemed to rather fizzle out. The ostensibly home-grown Free Speech Union initiative seemed to have a better chance because, like so many rightist culture war initiatives, it seems English, though there were actually *so many Americans involved*, and to have been there from the early days.

But there were problems from the start when the campaign went live in 2020. As Archie Bland reported in the *Guardian* in 2021, student free-speech activists around the country recruited to the non-partisan-sounding Free Speech Youth Advisory Board found it wasn't what they'd expected. Only *some* speech was really free for the new organisation's "right-of-centre orthodoxy". The rest was censored. And according to Bland, recruits were "dismayed" to realise that this admirable-sounding 'grassroots' initiative was actually a front for the FSU. That wasn't what they'd wanted. One said "organisations like the FSU are just perpetuating a culture war". Another said they "purposely hushed the FSU's involvement down". Just ahead of the planned launch "at least six" of the 16 founding participants had withdrawn.[170]

11 The New Elite

Are you in the New Elite, the one that apparently runs the country now, according to Professor Matthew Goodwin? They're terribly successful and they're all graduates with, at the very least, first degrees, often more. They've been to Russell Group universities – if not Oxbridge, of course. They've mostly come from smart, well-off backgrounds and they all know each other. In fact, they're mostly married to each other.

They've got all the top jobs in all the top places, particularly academics. *Especially academics.* It's more than my life's worth to spell out exactly what these jobs are, but they're tremendously top. So top indeed that they set the rules for everyone – including all the decent ordinary non-smart people who didn't go to university, don't live in London and don't have any top jobs, because they're not the New Elite.

You'll know if you're a member of this New Elite because you'll have had a charming little note *in code*, but because you're brought up in this sort of thing, you'll recognise it and then burn the little note. It may sound like a description of the younger members of, say, the Carlton Club, or people who go to Davos. But interestingly, it turns out that all these people are completely unlike such people in the past, and whether they studied Chemical Engineering, Theology or PPE, they're all wildly, indeed, *radically* progressive and they support all sorts of ultra-progressive things like Black Lives Matter, trans rights and the National Trust.

They support Extinction Rebellion and Just Stop Oil and they're forever gluing themselves to the public infrastructure. They've taken over the judiciary, the civil service and both main political parties. They control the media. And the City. They always ask you what your pronouns are. They're different from the Old Elites who, as you know, all had titles and lived in places that looked like Downtown Abbey. Or from the old super-rich – no names please – who had more money than the Queen!

The Old Elites had a sense of place, even if some of them were non-doms and lived in the South of France. They believed in this country and everything in it, including the businesses that aren't there any more, because the New Elites have sold them to foreigners. And they really cared about the ordinary decent people outside London who hadn't got university degrees or top jobs. They often wished those nice people would come back and look after them in their big houses – like their grandparents did. Sadly, now they have to bring in charming people from the Philippines and places like that. But the Old Elites did have a traditional work ethic, one which many ordinary people sadly may be losing because they're always preoccupied about whether to gender transition or take the knee, or welcome asylum seekers at the seashore rather than thinking about what's best for the nation and volunteering for national service.

This dramatic description of the UK's New Elites is the central conceit/Big Idea of Professor Matthew Goodwin's plangently titled *Values, Voice and Virtues*, published by Penguin on 30 March 2023. There are a lot of other expositions and analyses in the book but this is the one that matters, because in a world of culture wars propaganda, the most important thing is to tell people who to hate most. That's what the 1st Viscount Northcliffe, first owner of the *Daily Mail* and the *Mirror*, had as his guiding principle: "I give my readers a daily hate".[171] Professor Goodwin's analysis, like most of the speakers at the London National Conservatism Conference of 2023, is what's called *post-liberal*, so he's against *economic* liberals (globalists) and *cultural* liberals because they've let the nation down, big time.

This description of the New Elite is a very big initiative since it sets out to define the *particular* elites who right-wing post-liberals should fight against, and in turn ropes in a number of more particular culture wars issues they should contest. Broadly, they're the ones that the New Elites are said to espouse because they're so tremendously Radical and Progressive. Professor Goodwin cites them in the book and on the new-right platforms he's constantly mounting (they're all the subjects you'd expect – BLM, trans, asylum seekers, environmentalism, etc.).

I'm a market researcher by background, and like Professor Goodwin I've conducted lots of focus groups with all sorts of people who aren't remotely like me, all over the place. I've also spent quality time listening to academics – particularly in the sociology area – to help me think about groups and classes and – for my base commercial purposes – *market segments*. So I'm quite 'across' the issue of how informed people define elites. As a result, some things about Prof Goodwin's Big Idea strike me as just possibly a bit wobbly and overblown. They seem to strike some of his old peer group of academics in politics etc. as actively preposterous. To start with, it's unclear exactly who these people are, and how many of them there really are.

There were two crucial questions my brilliant first employer told me to ask about any alleged trend:

1. 'Who is actually doing it?' i.e. demographics, psychographics, the lot.
2. 'How many of them are there?'

The answers to these questions helped you decide whether the alleged trends warranted attention. A bit later on, I learnt the third and vital 'follow the money!' guidance. Meaning: who's funding it, and who's profiting from it?

On the first – who's doing the New Elites thing – Prof Goodwin's definitions and emphases tend to vary. There's a lot of focus on the public sector, particularly academics (yes, them again), NGOs, international organisations, activist lawyers, the civil service. And, to be fair, he does talk about business – particularly Big Business – whose key Davos-y leaders will, at a guess, have gone on from their smart first degrees to an MBA from London Business School, INSEAD in France or Harvard in the United States. Professor Goodwin has said that these people have no business foisting their radical progressive views on their companies' public positions. Apparently, they're forcing their people to take the knee on a constant basis when they're out in public and talking about non-binaryness and pronouns at every opportunity.

It's unclear exactly who is and isn't included in the private sector in Professor Goodwin's calculations. You would've thought that something like 99% of the City was liberal globalist in the economic sense – particularly hedge-funders – and belong in here, but he doesn't make much of them. He doesn't make much of the serious super-rich either – the people worth at least £100 million – proper plutocrats like, say, the billionaire Lord Bamford, who can do anything they like, including supporting Boris Johnson day and night. And, come to that, he's a bit sweeping and non-specific about media too, practically saying they've all gone New Elite radprog too, so that must mean the people at the *Mail* (the UK's bestselling newspaper) and its little friend the *Telegraph*. Or the *Sun* (Professor Goodwin writes for the *Spectator*, *Mail* and *Telegraph*, and he's written for the *Sun* too). I hadn't noticed somehow that these newspapers had gone completely RadProg.

Then there's government itself, which might include, apart from civil servants, Conservative Party MPs and the 172,000 party members who elect the PMs between elections. I hadn't noticed Mark Francois (look him up!) or Lee Anderson saying anything radprog. Nor the current Cabinet.

Given the uncertainties about the exact groups we are and aren't talking about here it's not surprising that Professor Goodwin's estimates of their actual number is *very* elastic, seeming to go from 12% of the population to 25% depending who he's talking to. Whatever it is, we're talking about huge numbers of people, too many people to constitute a proper seagoing Elite. Experts usually go for, at most, the top 10% but prefer 5%, and when they're talking about supermoney and superpower, tend to go for a fraction of the top 1% (the threshold income of the top 1% of UK earners is £183,000 pa).

That narrows it down a bit. If the *average* income of these tremendously successful, connected graduate people was, say, that £183,000 pa or so (we know some in academic, public sector etc. jobs may have to scrape by on anywhere between £75,000 and £100,000, which means they're only in the top 5% of the population). The top 1% consists of 685,500 people according to Oxfam's wealth report of January 2023.[172]

So it's worth going back to the original definitions and theories of eliteness. The ones that Prof Goodwin's academic peers would roll with; the ones Prof Goodwin's group should reasonably be compared with if he's saying it's all pukka in his bit of prof-land. The people who might be asked to peer-review other academics' work. One definition of an elite is that its members own/access huge multiples of ordinary people's access to financial capital, social capital (connectedness) and cultural power/influence, including media.

In the most recent 'big' class study of the UK conducted in 2013, by academics from six British universities backed by the BBC as the media partner,[173] the 'top' group in the seven-group hierarchy was the 'elite' class. *It was the top 6% of British society* and the average household income of this group was £89,000 back in 2011. It covers most of the tolerably well-educated, well-rewarded types you could identify (but Goodwin didn't). And then again, to get to the Goodwin level you'd have had to filter them for the radprog tendency. How many of these people – somewhere between the 5% and the 0.5% – are actually radprog enough. I know that two of Goodwin's targets – academia and media-land – are said to be and sometimes surveyed as being somewhat 'left' but how radprog exactly is that?

I talked to some academics in the politics and sociology areas to understand how they viewed Professor Goodwin's central concept of the New Elite.

Professor Sam Friedman is Professor of Sociology at the London School of Economics. He has published widely on class, culture and social mobility. He has a particular interest in elites and elitism. His *The Class Ceiling: Why it Pays to be Privileged* of 2020, co-written with Daniel Laurison, describes how class/background influences people's career outcomes (it's particularly amusing about the hypocrisy of media organisations!).

His *Born to Rule: The Making and Remaking of the British Elite* (co-written with Aaron Reeves) will be published in September 2024. In it Reeves and Friedman analyse a mass of historic data from *Who's Who* to identify – and quantify – people who have roles/jobs that have real influence and power. They combined this with other material – probate records, etc. – about wealth to get some idea of who the current British elite – whether 'old' or 'new' – might be.

Friedman reckons that there are about 6,000 people in the UK who qualify by virtue of their combination of positional and economic power – i.e. they are both included in *Who's Who* and are in the top 1% of the wealth distribution. He thinks Professor Goodwin's definition is much too wide and much too vague: "The concept of a New Elite is just too fuzzy. How can 25% of the population – some seventeen million people – occupy positions of immense economic, political and cultural power. The numbers just don't add up," he says.

And when we look at the big political picture how many academics (or students for that matter) in the largest disciplines are radprog? Take, say, Business Studies, Medicine, Engineering, etc. What percentage are radprog there, would you think? And as for journalists being RP, what matters in terms of output and influence are senior editors and proprietors. If we think across the very small range of such people in, say, the British national press, and partic-ularly the four businesses that account for more than 90% of UK newspaper sales, how many radprogs are there at the very top, the people who say what goes?! (And before anyone mentions the *Guardian*, it's worth saying it's only about 2.17% of UK daily print circulation!)[174]

116

Rob Ford is Professor of Political Science at Manchester University, and a former collaborator with Matthew Goodwin on a number of projects, especially their very prescient book of 2013, *Revolt on the Right*. I'd admired it when it came out, describing people who felt, in David Goodhart's words, "left behind". I often felt later how very predictive it had been.

Professor Ford told me: "Goodwin's New Elites concept is far too vague and broadly defined to be useful. Goodwin's New Elite is not really an elite and often not really new either. The term encompasses a random grab-bag of individuals, institutions and social groups whose only common features are political views Goodwin dislikes. Serious research furnishes us with clear, well-defined concepts and arguments, not boo-phrases thrown around in arbitrary fashion to signal disapproval."

When I asked Ford whether the constituent groups in the New Elite really welded power, he said:

"A concept of 'elite' which includes a young university graduate struggling to make rent, but excludes the owners of the nation's most influential newspapers and MPs from the party which has run the country for the last decade, is hard to take seriously. But the goal of the New Elites thesis is political, not explanatory. Goodwin is not making a serious effort to understand the world, but is instead pursuing a political agenda, laying out a framework for identifying friends and enemies. 'The People' encompasses everyone who shares his views. The 'New Elite' encompasses anyone who disagrees.

"This desire to oppose a 'pure people' and a 'corrupt elite' is a fairly standard move in radical right politics, a world Goodwin has studied for decades. It seems he is now putting the lessons of his research into practice, by developing his own radical right political agenda, complete with its own roster of heroes and rogues' gallery of villains."

Professor Goodwin (I don't know whether he still does the usual hours in in the usual ways at the University of Kent), is now a very considerable entrepreneur and media face published, in this case, by a major publisher, Penguin. He's on every right-wing stage, platform and panel going. He writes for the newspapers. He's on GB News and Talk TV. Back in 2018 the Legatum Institute appointed Prof Goodwin as the founding director of the Centre for UK Prosperity.[175] It sounded completely splendid and as if it might be very well rewarded too (although that doesn't seem to figure in the coverage). But it didn't last; in less than a year they'd shut up shop and no one concerned ever seems to have mentioned it again.

However Prof Goodwin does have a consultancy company called People Polling which gives research-based advice to presumably elite – but not radprog – business decision-takers. These various developments would suggest that his income has very significantly improved over the last ten years (oh, and he's got a growing Substack too).

But the greatest change is in what he says. He's gone from the careful analyst – even a rather centrist sounding one – of the kind displayed in, say, his *New Statesman* article of November 2013 where he warned, "Why the immigration debate is getting us nowhere. The more we stoke public anger and distraction on immigration, the more we threaten the stability of our political system in general." But now he's plunged into all those debates in support of the populist right.

In the text, he says of the voters' defection to more extreme minority groups, "Those on the margins will celebrate; but those in the more moderate majority should be deeply worried." Now, however, he is definitely in the 'Family, flag and faith' world – the one he spoke to in such decidedly stirring ways at NatCon on 19 March 2023.

Professor Goodwin's speech at the 2023 National Conservatism Conference was highly dramatic. He accused the Conservatives of economic liberalism and the Labour party of cultural liberalism. The majority of Brits, so he implied, didn't want either; these views were only shared by 20% of the population (presumably the New Elite radprogs), so he said. The implication being that we'd be better off with a more nationalistic set-up. His critique of the Conservative governments after 2010 was forensic and he went on to say the only people accorded honour in the country now were "minorities and their graduate allies". All the rest, and particularly white working-class men, were held in low esteem. A number of people, who didn't want to be quoted, suggested that Professor Goodwin might be interested in a role in the new configuration on the right that is emerging after the election.

12 Trans: How the Cat Led Us to the Ladies' Loos

Who chooses Piers Morgan's subjects for his internationally linked programmes on his YouTube channel Piers Morgan Uncensored? Morgan's global deal with NewsCorp is said to be worth £50 million over three years and makes him easily the UK's best-paid broadcast journalist. Whenever I watch Piers Morgan Uncensored they seem to be talking about trans this and trans that, as if the transgender issues were the most important in the Anglosphere (Morgan's deal particularly covers the UK, the US – Fox News – and Australia – Sky News Australia).

Why is he doing it, or being directed to do it? Do his editors think it generates ratings, or do they have a corporate axe to grind? Or does Murdoch himself have one? Apparently, he was deeply involved in the Morgan deal.[176]

If you were a real person watching Morgan constantly, you just might end up thinking his commentary on transgender issues has all gone a bit far. You'd certainly get the impression that thousands of men were declaring themselves to be women every day. And that now this declaration was all they had to do to 'change sex', as people used to call it. In an earlier time, we'd all heard that people who wanted to 'gender reassign', had to do a fair bit and spend a decent amount of time to get their application endorsed and their documents changed.

Two years' solid living as someone of 'the other sex' was what most people think they remember from 20th-century coverage. And then, for men, the chop. But now we're being told constantly it's the thought that counts, the conviction that mind and spirit are what matters, while biology was a lower-order concern. Or that would've been your takeaway from Morgan's performance as the plain man in the Home Counties saloon bar.

But when exactly did that cat come into our calculations about human gender? There'd always been a line of British humour left over from Bernard Manning – or Jim Davidson perhaps – when same-sex marriage was being debated here, back in March 2012, where the joke would be about marrying your Labrador next. And Morgan's view seems to derive from this 'whatever next?' view of the world.

But that cat, originally cited in news stories in the week of 18 June 2023,[177] didn't seem to have come from paleo-comedians but a film of real British girls in a Home Counties school (Rye College in East Sussex) apparently talking about a girl who seriously thought she was a cat – who *identified* as one (there was no cat-girl, so it turned out – this was actually Year 8 doing a bit of a hypothetical).[178]

Suddenly the story was everywhere, because the shadowy media unit that trawls for stories suggesting that the woke mob were turning young people quite mad – so mad indeed that the foundations of future national sanity were under threat – had got onto it. The anti-woke brigade knew exactly what it was all about. *'Cat' was a proxy for trans, obvs*. And we were constantly being told that all you had to do to transition now was to identify, to declare, *to speak your inner truth*, and in no time, you'd be handed the keys to everything – the ladies' lavs in Claridge's, membership of the national women's Olympic swimming team, the lot.

Whatever it was, it was a viral TikTok that got it going. And one in which a girl seems to compare cat-identification to the whole touchy business of human gender identity. This, in turn, seemed to provoke a teacher to start spouting some fatuous stuff about there being lots of genders – and to say the girls' views were despicable. *That did it*. The exchange was in the *Sun* and the *Mail* in two flicks of a cat's tail.[179] The Good and the Great were now routinely quizzed on this subject; could people transition to cat status just like that? Or indeed could anyone transition to *anything* just like that?

The Great were called in to comment. A spokesman for the prime minister said it was "not right for children to be influenced by the 'personal views' of teachers when it comes to transgender issues" (*Daily Mail*).[180] Keir Starmer said something typically cautious: "I think children should be told to identify as children" (*The Guardian*),[181] and the equalities minister, Kemi Badenoch, never shy of a rumble, waded in to say there should be an Ofsted inspection of the school because there seemed to be a teacher turning tiny minds with woke propaganda (teachers turning tiny minds is the theme of a raft of culture wars sorties).[182]

If you've been watching US culture wars online over the last decade like me, you'd know that *the lavs have it*. Over the last decade, evangelical right-wing Republicans couldn't stop talking about what they see as the clear and present danger of trans women invading women's single-sex spaces. To innocent liberals who say it doesn't seem to have happened yet – trans people overall are more often the victims of crime than the perpetrators[183] – they have a ready answer, much like Zhou Enlai's answer about the French Revolution: *it's too early to say*. They're constantly pushing the line that the so-called 'trans ideology' that's pushing people to change gender, and legislation that will supposedly make it so much easier to do, will vastly increase the numbers of people at the door of the Ladies'. And they'll practically all have penises this time. They'll have changed on a whim, or something worse – they'll have changed gender over-whelmingly because they want to *get close* to women. They see this as a nifty way to spy on them as pervy voyeurs, or to rape them. *That's the story.*

There's a whole group of women's single-sex spaces to worry about, we're told. Prison, for a start, where genitally intact trans women could clearly wreak havoc. Or women's refuges where men would pass themselves off as battered partners just to get in and do their worst. And then there's sport: no one wants hulking men who've been through male puberty – whether equipped with working willies or not – riding, jumping and swimming in competition with cis women. It's unfair just when, for instance, women were doing so well in sport (much has been made of an American trans swimmer called Lia Thomas who is apparently six foot four and is apparently intact, winning against women every time).[184] And what about the changing rooms? You wouldn't want your sporty daughter changing with a 6'4" 'bloke' would you? The idea of trans women in those places makes even the most rational, tolerant women anxious, though they might not want to acknowledge it. And their rational partners, who know perfectly well *that other men are beasts* pick up on those worries.

But anyone who knows the reality of the majority of men who seriously want to change gender – to be MTF, let's forget the female-to-male group for the moment – will know that it's not a thing anyone does on a whim. It's not an overnight transition, whatever the formal process. It involves years of depression and suppression and shame long before they're accepted into *any* kind of therapy – let alone any transition process. Before anyone pays attention. All this background is well documented in, say, Shon Faye's *The Transgender Issue*. Any clinical/therapeutic account – no matter how political – acknowledges that trans women are a *very* small group in the population. The consensus is well under 1% of women and arguably far fewer, and most of them have a very hard time.

According to many 'gender-critical' accounts, a majority of young trans women – older transitions are different – would have gone on to be gay men if an 'intervention' hadn't been encouraged. It's the encouraging that's caused all the fuss. The story is that there's a hugely important, powerful politicised subgroup in the trans lobby that's taken over the institutions. They're, naturally, a subset of the woke mob that's taken over the world. And that's where the politics, the big money and the big media come in.

Helen Joyce is a former senior *Economist* staff writer with an impressive maths background who's written a successful book called *Trans: When Ideology Meets Reality* (2021).[185] It's successful in terms of sales, and hyper-successful in terms of *coverage*. She's been on every right-leaning TV programme, YouTube channel and podcast around the Anglosphere. And now she's out there with a purpose, having left the *Economist* for a campaigning organisation called Sex

Matters. *Joyce is saying, twice daily, that trans women are a danger to 'real' ones and that the 'gender-affirming' processes that trans people go through are harmful to them.* You're meant to feel concerned. In a sophisticated way she seems to be endorsing '30p Lee' Anderson in his belief that trans issues might just be an election winner this year. The right-leaning talking shops she's been on include:

- The Rubin Report
- Triggernometry
- Gript Media
- Peter Boghossian
- Talk TV
- GB News
- The Spectator TV
- Women's Declaration International
- The Signal
- Heretics Clips
- The IEA Channel (YouTube)
- Keep Talking Podcast
- The Free Speech Union
- Jordan Peterson Clips
- along with more 'mainstream' programming like *Good Morning Britain.*

Which says to me that Joyce seems to be what the doctor ordered for a very definable political interest. Hers is a campaigning group that supports TERFS (trans-exclusionary radical feminists) and, understandably, worries parents with the thought that 'gay children are being sterilised'.[186]

We've heard endlessly now about transgender *affirming* in gender identity clinics (GIDs) – how apparently any teenage boy who goes there with worrying thoughts will end up being a trans girl. For Brits it's focused on a famous UK example – the Tavistock GID, a long-established subset of an even longer-established NHS specialist mental health clinic in thoughtful North London (at Swiss Cottage, gateway to Hampstead, ground zero for the liberal elite!). The debate has been whether some staff in the Tavistock GID – and 'activists' elsewhere –

were dangerously doctrinaire in their keenness to see troubled teens change sex. The numbers don't seem to bear this out whatever those staffers views were. The number of applicants for help increased enormously over the last decade, especially among girls wanting to transition to being boys. However, the percentage of even the Tavistock's patients emerging as fully transitioned with hormones and surgery seems pretty small.[187]

Underneath Joyce's upper-middle-class media-friendly articulation, the Sex Matters message seemed viscerally clear. First, trans women constituted a clear and present danger to cis women in lavs, prisons and refuges. Second, in ways that were sometimes difficult to follow, they were a threat to the traditional women's movement, to feminists and especially to lesbians (trans women were allegedly trying to hook up with lesbians on dating sites and stick their intact penises in them, whether they wanted it or not).[188] And trans women were unfair competition in sport.

It was interesting to see how a subgroup of notable feminists, some of them lesbians, had apparently come to see trans women as their primary enemy. Just how representative this subgroup was nobody really knew, but there was some important but very confusing in-group language on either side. The thoughtful anti-trans women were called TERFS by the trans rights activists. Ordinary people without skin in the game asked how vanishingly small a subset of womankind those acronyms could be defining (and did they all *teach in schools or universities?!*). The anti-trans league, in turn, called themselves 'gender-critical'! What this meant was that they rejected the big idea of subjective gender as the key factor in deciding who you really were, rather than basic biological sex – chromosomes, genital configuration at birth, etc.

There were some high-profile, big-platform characters created by the debate. Kathleen Stock, a former philosophy professor at the University of Sussex, said she had been forced out of her job in 2021 by the trans-activists, who included Sussex students, for insisting publicly on what she deemed to be the "common-sense" answer to this great question of sex v gender in 2021. Thereafter the 'gotcha' question posed constantly to leftish politicians by right-leaning presenters was 'What is a woman?'.

It was an astonishing takedown and dreadful to watch. Politicians with PhDs spluttered into incoherence, trying to find something that would please everyone and avoid TERF talking points. Stock herself, generally seen as left leaning and certainly someone who constantly identified herself on platforms as a feminist and a lesbian, became a convenient martyr for media platforms of precisely the kind which would've happily hatcheted her existence, let alone her views, ten years before. Not only were all women at risk from the trans mob, so she said, but lesbian lefties were also especially threatened. *Culture wars create very strange bedfellows* because they aim to identify and exploit tensions in the target group. So there was Stock on Talk TV with sympathetic-sounding Julia Hartley-Brewer – hardly an obvious supporter for a leftish lesbian feminist.[189]And there she was on UnHerd, Sir Paul Marshall's libertarian-right site, saying to the camera and the microphone, "I won't be silenced."[190] She'd gone full martyr.

After she resigned from Sussex in 2021, Stock was involved in a variety of initiatives like Channel 4's *Gender Wars* (broadcast *in May 2023* and so criticised by its other trans participants that Channel 4 has withdrawn it from streaming) and the Lesbian Project, "intended to put lesbian needs and interest back into focus; to stop lesbians disappearing in rainbow soup".[191] She also joined the University of Austin, Texas, a new institution only certified *in October 2023* with no students enrolled yet, but with a number of high-profile media conservatives (Ayan Hirsi Ali, Andrew Sullivan, etc.) on its founders group. Stock, described as a faculty fellow, didn't have to move an inch; she could contribute remotely. All this didn't stop the Austin people from staging a debate/discussion involving her for YouTube in September 2023 in a grand hall somewhere that looked vaguely like Congress. This well-endowed *liberal arts college* put on this interesting show before it officially existed and a year before it enrolled any undergraduate students.

The question here absolutely isn't about the virtues of the

arguments on either side but about who's paying to push them and why. Stock broadly says the same things as Joyce, who *isn't* a feminist or a lesbian, and from the indications – she's very articulate and careful to cover off anything too explicitly party political – not exactly a leftist either. The point is, they're going at this issue full tilt, pressing every alarm button going about the mobs that have apparently taken over the nation. They're promoting the issues posed by a tiny unimportant group to constant soundbite status.

In October 2019, two mature lesbians, Bev Jackson and Kate Harris, set up the LGB Alliance, a group of lesbians and gay men – more of the first – whose ostensible objective was "to advance lesbian, gay and bisexual rights". However, it seemed in practice to be mainly concerned to exclude trans people – by conspicuously cutting off the usual T for a start. The gender-critical Kathleen Stock is a patron of the LGB Alliance.

In a case brought by Mermaids, a pro-trans charity, to appeal the Charity Commission awarding charity status to the LGB Alliance,[192] Paul Roberts, the chief executive of LGBT Consortium, a network of LGBT organisations, said in evidence that they believed that the LGB Alliance had been exclusively concerned with promoting anti-trans and gender-critical beliefs, lobbying for legal change in favour of their views and pushing back against organisations that advocate in favour of 'trans equality'.

In November 2021 the veteran LGBT+ rights campaigner Peter Tatchell had written: "I oppose the trans-critical views of Kathleen Stock and others." He went on to say:

> In the early 1970s, a battle cry of the women's liberation movement was 'biology is NOT destiny'. Now some trans-critical feminists are saying 'biology IS destiny'. A regressive step, I think. Biology is a reality but progressives should be doing everything in their power to limit its adverse consequences for both women and trans people.

Bev Jackson and Kate Harris's veteran gay leftish campaigning credentials seemed immaculate so it was interesting to read in *Byline Times* that their organisation was headquartered in... *55 Tufton*

Street.[193] *No one is headquartered in 55 Tufton Street by accident.* It is a political collective headquarters inhabited by far-right pressure groups and think tanks – organisations which work in lockstep, according to Shahmir Sanni, a former TaxPayers' Alliance employee. It isn't like a WeWork. No campaigning organisation would find itself there just by asking an estate agent.

A recent *Newsnight* report of 20 March 2024 claimed people looking for NHS 'gendercare' are facing years-long waits.[194] The BBC analysis found it could take ten years to clear the backlog of people waiting for first appointments. They interviewed the mother of 20-year-old Alice Litman who killed herself while waiting for treatment. Mrs Litman said, "There is no care for trans-people." A Department of Health spokesperson said they were facing "unpredictable demand".

However the new conservative media circuit – particularly GB News and Talk TV, the two TV channels then competing to be the UK's leading right-wing influencer, the Fox News of Britain – had convenient voices saying that the trans mob is at the door of every women's safe space. And they ran with it. They were getting third-party endorsement from these clever donnish types like Stock and Joyce.

What exactly is it that leads disgruntled soft-left people – particularly academics – to open their hearts like this on right-wing media and conference platforms where they're so obviously preaching to the converted? It's difficult making out who these hugely powerful trans-activists are (no doubt Lee Anderson knows), but if you think they really *exist* in your world, or your institution, *why aren't you arguing it out somewhere else*, in halls and platforms where you're not sponsored (sometimes paid too) by people who you would've condemned a few years ago – and not speaking to closed minds? Shouldn't your PR be making a few calls to the open-minded undecided. The culture warriors have weaponised the trans story at the expense of a host of private struggles. They've invented a ubiquitous group of trans-activists and got talking heads everywhere talking away. Meanwhile, dead cat style, we're not really looking at anything else.

In April 2024 the Cass Review, an independent review of gender identity services for children and young people commissioned by the NHS in 2020, was published, all 290 pages of it.[195] The chair of the review group, Dr Hilary Cass OBE (honorary consultant paediatrician at Evelina London Children's Hospital, Guy's & St Thomas's NHS Foundation Trust), set a deliberately cool tone in defining the objectives and the context: "This Review is not about what it means to be trans." It was simply "about what the healthcare approach should be".

The context was that this was "an arena where there were strong and widely divergent opinions unsupported by adequate evidence". There was "an increasingly toxic, ideological and polarised public debate" (in other words barking). They concluded that the evidence base from which current approaches derived was weak, with a lot of misinformation easily accessible online.

They set out the background numbers of children and young people seeking help from the UK NHS GIDs since 2009 – before that the service saw fewer than 50 children a year. There had been an exponential rise in 2014 and by 2016 the pattern of referrals showed the increase had disproportionately been seen in "birth registered females presenting in adolescence". In 2016 there'd been 1,071 adolescent girls and 426 adolescent boys, i.e. more than twice as many girls. But all the fuss, from gender-critical pressure groups and newspapers and celebrities, had overwhelmingly been about male-to-female transitioning, demonising trans women in all sorts of ways.

The actual referrals – boys and girls – displayed a huge variety of physical and mental health situations. The review concluded that they deserved to be assessed and treated *individually*. But they'd been let down, so the evidence showed, by the widespread adoption of new approaches with inadequate analysis or safeguards. For whatever reason GIDs had "abandoned normal clinical approaches to holistic assessment".

The Cass Review took some of the heat out of the situation with its intelligent analysis (but, for the critics, it confirmed the view that there had been a trans ideology at work). As the report said, a review of healthcare practice for children and adolescents couldn't determine the ways trans people should be treated politically.

To return to Peter Tatchell's point that the rights of women, gay people and trans people *are* part of the same struggle: he believes that LGB and T *do* belong together.[196] He says the gender-critical (or anti-trans) groups take tiny examples – behaviour or rhetoric – and blow them up into sweeping generalisations about all trans people. Trans women, so he says, have been using women's toilets for ages with no ill effects for anyone. The idea that intending rapists see a trans identity as an easy route to voyeurism and rape is inherently absurd; why would they bother when conventional rapes usually went unpunished? The talking points used against trans women now, so he says, were the ones used against gay rights – and especially same-sex marriage rights – that he'd seen over the last 40+ years.

Tatchell had recently been in touch with Kemi Badenoch, the then UK equalities minister,[197] prompted by her saying that she'd met "extensively" with numerous LGBT+ groups. He believed she hadn't, that she'd only met the anti-trans groups – Helen Joyce's Sex Matters and Transgender Trend. He offered to facilitate a round-table discussion with a wider group including the UK's longer-standing LGBT+ groups. She replied saying, very clearly, thanks but no thanks.[198] She'd met the people who mattered – who were "constructive and collaborative" – and she was too busy to meet anyone else.

13 A Tale of One City

We all know, in principle, how dominant London is, how much bigger and richer than other UK cities. But if we live and work outside the 100-mile city-state many of us would rather not think too much about it (full disclosure, I'm a lifetime Londoner). When it comes to the culture war players though, London's dominance is *absolute*. The entire secret confederacy of professions and powers is all packed into just a few square miles of London.

'And where do *you* live?' is an absolutely key question for any of us raised in the wonderful world of marketing. Or more precisely, *market research*, where I had my first proper job. My first – and last – employer was a brilliant American who'd done Philosophy at Harvard and loved Britain. He'd come here in the late 60s and stayed. Smartly married and Chelsea-housed, he'd become a market research entrepreneur by the mid 70s. He'd had a clear brand proposition for the business; he did *smart, clever* research – rather than just numbers – and for smart, clever clients: the growing design sector or clever publishers like the *FT*.

Our outfit chased and explained trends. Our offices were in a smart, clever cream stucco house in Belgravia, in the heart of everything and up the road from Parliament. From there we set out on constant expeditions to understand the nation's secret heart. We aimed to understand what people from Bury to Berwick, Plymouth to Peebles really knew about anything. We specialised in clever follow-up questions – the ones to determine why people said the things they did. 'And why do you think that?' was a staple – bland and unchallenging, it would help you determine whether your respondent had any real/direct knowledge of whatever it was or whether they were just parroting a tabloid headline. This experience meant I rapidly came to the view that *a combination of class and geography* was still destiny in the 1970s.

In the late 70s a new kind of database service – the generic category is termed *geo-demographics* – called ACORN was launched by the marketing consultancy CACI,[199] It combined the new computational power then becoming available with a range of public (e.g. the census) and private databases to give ever more precise pictures of the people in ever smaller focused areas – enumeration districts within postcodes. This showed, broadly, that birds of a feather really did flock together. You are where you live. ACORN meant that if you knew someone's postcode you could predict an awful lot about them without ever getting in contact. It was hugely useful then for focusing advertising and direct mail spend. This made your customer and prospect address lists absolute gold dust.

This century, when the internet hosted the extraordinarily scary power of the Silicon Valley empires, it looked as if digital natives with money would get to know everything about everyone. But equally, there was the persistent idealistic turn-of-the-century Berners-Lee belief that the internet would allow everyone everywhere to know everything about their world and their masters. It would be a great leveller, with the happy expectation that people wouldn't get fooled again. The world would become a fact-checked paradise of shared rationality, one huge BBC Verify. All the things we now call culture wars would wither away.

It didn't work out like that. Anyone who's seen MAGA followers talking about, say, QAnon, or Brexiteers talking about their version of the Great Replacement Theory (31% of Brexit voters believe that international conspiracy theory but only 6% of Remainers),[200] soon realised that the internet generally and social media in particular can be used by propagandists to sell new and old lies – some dating back to Tsarist inventions, many to top Nazi Joseph

Goebbels' playbook. Conspiracy believers are forever telling sceptics that they've 'done their research'. But by the time they were doing 'research' the internet was chock full of elephant traps for the unwary – and here's where we get to the massively sensitive question of what research means for the not very connected, the not very metropolitan and the not very well educated.

By the time Trump was up for election in 2016, the online traps were set – some by Trump's fanboy favourite Vladimir Putin (check it out!).[201] The right-wing newspapers and magazines were developing impressive online presences. And there was a mass of online astroturf, much of it with anonymous or fraudulent origins.

So, a combination of class and geography remained as powerful as ever in influencing and understanding people's loyalties. The renewed sensitivity about class in the populist age was often focused on education. The most enthusiastic MAGAs – the 6th January rioters – weren't unemployed car workers or West Virginia miners. Some were distinctly well off, so the analyses of the arrests showed.[202] But there were clues in their profiles about *educational class and geography*. They weren't young Ivy Leaguers from the US North-East (for comparison the analysis of UKIP enthusiasts here showed a preponderance of older white working-class men, but not the very poorest 10%).

What populists everywhere always call the 'metropolitan' liberal elite – better-educated big-city professional people – and, in the UK, overwhelmingly *Londoners*, tend to be significantly more 'liberal', sceptical about the culture war themes and about the conspiracy theories. The UK is a wildly unbalanced country where literally everything that matters to the 'players' happens in London and is resented. 'Liberal' Londoners who get involved in the culture wars know what a minefield that 'metropolitan' tag is.

All the achingly elite and often obscure occupations that matter in the culture wars operate overwhelmingly, if not exclusively, in London. If you live and work in provincial Britain (by German or American standards our 'big' second cities are small), it's another world.

So where *do* you live? And where do you *work*? And is it your home town? Where are you *connected*? Unless it's London/one of its Home Counties dormitories, you'll probably never have come across a whole range of perfectly legal culture wars endeavours or know anyone who works in them.

What do you know about the workings of

- hedge-fund trading
- political/economic think tanks
- private-equity businesses
- political lobbyists
- City/financial PRs
- 'SPADS' (parliamentary special advisors)
- senior national newspapers' political and 'comment' editors
- national broadcasters' news management?

And who do you know who works in those occupations?

Practically all these exotic jobs are carried out in a few square miles of central London – in the City and the borough of Westminster, with a scattering in the adjacent borough of Kensington and Chelsea. (K&C and Westminster are also, of course, the two richest boroughs in the country.)

If you live a normal British life – from farmers to GPs to lorry drivers or call centre workers – outside London's '100-mile city' you know perfectly well that all the visible Big Stuff happens in London; there's central government, monarchy, high finance, national media national arts institutions, the creative industries (when they're at scale) and every kind of other national institution that's grown out of imperial London since the 1850s.

But no one could blame you for *not* knowing, say, how political think tanks operate with their lobbyist clients and their parliamentary friends including government ministers and the political editors of national newspapers. Get a life! It's an obsessive, geeky preoccupation.

But those people in those exotic incestuous interlinked London occupational bubbles are hugely interested in *you* – in psephology (the quantitative analysis of elections and balloting!) and demography and every kind of political technology that could help them understand and manipulate your opinions. They want your useful skills and your votes. They want your support. But they don't usually want to spend any more time with you than they absolutely have to.

In David Goodhart's widely quoted *Road to Somewhere*, the distinction between the two groups he called Somewheres and Anywheres is central. The Anywheres – educated people with globally saleable skills and globally liberal opinions (as he sees them) – tend to be disproportionately packed into London. In any class analysis you can muster, London has more of the top 5% (and the top 1%). So it's hardly surprising that Anywhere members – disproportionately privately educated, Oxbridge trained, etc. – find themselves working in those culture wars jobs there.

The right constantly says the left is waging all the culture wars – in the playground style of 'he started it'. Indeed they always claim that the left have already won so many of them that ordinary decent people must fight back. They've won – so the story goes – in precisely those places, and those institutions like the universities and the senior civil service that most of the nation barely understands (so you can make up anything you like about them). We're talking here about the magic kingdom of the liberal elite again, especially the metropolitan liberal elite. This group features wildly in the illiberal imagination and in their narratives. However, it never really has a name or an address attached, so you can make it up as you go along. So it was that a very approximate collection of liberal celebrities and leftie lawyers (a favourite term with the Tory Cabinet), crazy wokist profs and eco-warrior environmentalists, became described as the 21st-century version of the 'masters of the universe' – Tom Wolfe's marvellous 80s term for the emerging kings of Wall Street who were happy with the attention back then.

But this irritating-sounding group *never* really ran the show. Never will. As anyone who really knows the score will tell you, none of these met-lib straw men matches the motivation, money and political power of, say, Rupert Murdoch (net worth $18 billion) or Peter Thiel (net worth $7.2 billion). No City titan would consider, say, Gary Lineker *seriously rich*. No media proprietor would *privately* consider, say, an academic with some TV profile or a vocal human-rights lawyer had anything like his power – direct access to any government assured – let alone his money. They support the narrative that a collection of cultural Marxists really runs the show, because people have lost the plot about who actually does, and that really suits the professional cultural warriors. *But they don't believe it for a minute.*

It used to be easier to identify the ruling class. Plutocrats were the people whose names were above the factory doors and aristocrats were named after the county. They were visible and known. Now fewer and fewer people really know who really owns the business they work for. A private-equity outfit can be based wherever it likes, with a distant and shadowy ownership structure. Conglomerates' legal centres shift with global tax regimes. And so often now you could be working at arms-length from your employer – either as a middle-class freelance or as a precariat/working-class gig economy worker.

So those national certainties about who's running the show at any level have disappeared. The right has rebooted a host of 60s/70s leftist styles and rhetoric, – 'Power to the people!' – because everyone's an anti-establishment rebel now, and no one more so than rich populists. If you're 'doing your research', always follow the money (Jacob Rees-Mogg is allegedly worth in excess of £100 million when combined with his wife's inheritance. His business was headquartered in Dublin, a sensible move for a Brexiteer who's also a player. (According to Tortoise Media, Somerset Capital Management called it quits in December 2023 after the value of its investments fell below £1 billion, down from £10 billion five years ago.)[203]

Part 2

Places & People

Behind Closed Doors

Imagine, for one sparkling moment that you were a *real* person. Someone who'd got quite enough to worry about keeping their job, putting food on the table, looking after their children and keeping up with their friends to think much about politics and politicians or following the Westminster gossip. Or to read the political magazines and watch BBC2's *Newsnight* five nights a week.

Just imagine, for one sparkling moment, that you also lived and worked 24/7 in a *real* place, well away from Westminster: Rotherham or Hartlepool, Plymouth or Paisley. It would be unlikely – not impossible – that you could confidently explain what any of the *unreal* people – the speccy geeks with the global connections who worked in that London SW1 world –actually *did*.

Even if you did know a bit, follow it online (which would make you that bit geeky and untypical), it would be vanishingly unlikely that you'd actually know anyone who really *did* any of those things as a job in your hood.

It's all about London! And we're not talking about the boroughs of Enfield or Barking and Dagenham. We're talking overwhelmingly about people who work in the City of London, or the boroughs of Kensington and Chelsea or Westminster – respectively the richest and second richest boroughs in the country. That narrows the field a bit. Think tank land for instance is clustered round Parliament, at the heart of Westminster. Lobbyists tend to have their offices there or thereabouts too. It's a sort of industrial logic. Lobbyists are retained in confidence by anyone from, say, an American multinational with a wish to acquire one or another part of our crumbling publicly owned infrastructure and make it private and profitable, or a sad beleaguered billionaire plutocrat convinced that he and his peers pay too much tax or their businesses suffer from too much regulation. Let's be clear: lobbyists can only be retained a) by people or organisations who won't face opposition within, i.e. absolute bosses and b) people who've got enormous amounts of money, people who can pay anywhere between hundreds of thousands and tens of millions to get their case across to government, to influencers and to the voting public.

It's not just the cost of the lobbyists – the people who think through the strategies for their clients – but the cost of the therapies they recommend. Lobbyists, according to commentators, talk about the opaquely funded right-wing think tanks as 'wonk whores'.[204] That's because, if they funnel a nice wedge of their clients' money to a suitable think-tank, they'll produce a report arguing their case – a 'third-party endorsement' from apparently unconnected clever dicks who seem a bit academic and researchy. And then spokespeople from the think tank go on TV and radio and online and in newspapers to argue their case. Most hard-worked broadcasting researchers are glad of someone to fill their screens and airwaves and they're not bothered to establish who's paid for this interesting report (either that or they're best mates or former colleagues in the wonderful revolving-door land of political Westminster).

The other thing the more modern, American-influenced lobbyists do is to invent and support an astroturf organisation that looks rooted in a locality or a community but isn't really. They've been dreamt up, directed and peopled with 'extras' by yet more clever folk in... Westminster. Astroturf groups, as we've seen, are called things you can't argue with like Mothers for Morality or Concerned Citizens of Land's End for X and they have compellingly real-seeming yet fiercely articulate spokespeople whose precise addresses are sometimes uncertain.

The fact is that, even now, only 0.05% of sentient British adult humanity knows anything substantial about these exotic London organisations (and the organisations like it that way). *But they've got their eyes on you.*

They want to get inside your head. They want to influence your opinions and your voting. In the following pieces I'm going to be taking you behind some of these influential but discreet London 'doors', starting with the heart of things in SW1, Conservative HQ.

Door 1
4 Matthew Parker Street

No. 4 Matthew Parker Street SW1 is an impressive late imperial (1914) building dominating the corner of this short Edwardian street round the side and back of the great Westminster Central Hall, highpoint of Methodist glory, itself completed in 1911. No 4 and the Central Hall were both designed by the architectural firm of Lanchester and Rickards, though in different styles. In Pevsner's Westminster volume he says brusquely, "Number 4 is by Lanchester and Rickards with a big shaped gable." The facade, in red brick, is sincere pastiche designed for *Forsyte Saga* taste with a strong oversized 'William and Mary' gable.

No. 4 is Conservative Campaign Headquarters, running the party which currently has 172,437 members who pay £39 a year to belong. This isn't enough to manage on for a modern party of the right, so they now have to seek other sources of support. These have been substantial, and have been documented in *Byline Times*.[205] (They raised more than £12 million in the first three months of 2023, including £5 million from Egyptian-born Mohamed Mansour and £2 million each from Indian-born Amit Lohia and from water company magnate Graham Edwards.)

The later donations from Frank Hester, much discussed in March 2024 since his disobliging remarks about Diane Abbott, were £15 million in all.[206]

Interior pictures of No. 4 suggest very considerable renovations before the Conservatives moved here in 2014 from 30 Millbank. So much so as to suggest the building might even have been 'facaded'

– i.e. rebuilt behind the retained period facade, symbolically hinting that Conservatives are less Conservative. A feel for the interior style can be gained from the 14 December 2021 video of a party for London mayoral candidate Shaun Bailey[207] (now Baron Bailey of Paddington after PM Johnson's resignation list). This was unearthed by newspapers to widespread criticism a year later. It featured in the 'Partygate' dossier.

But what do we make of the interior design and the dress codes on display here? What exactly *is* the Conservative Party now and what goes on in the roughly 20,000 square feet of the ground and basement they occupy?

The Conservative Party was founded in 1834. It is widely described as being the most continuously successful political party in the world. There is a conventional wisdom that this success derives from its raging pragmatism – meaning that it's not overly troubled by ideologies (or unbreakable principles?). Rather, it does what's necessary to stay in power. But a lack of ideology hasn't, historically, meant Tories are totally untethered and unpredictable. They believed in their people and – again historically – an idea of a social architecture. Their people have been toffs and then aspirant plutocrats as the world changed. The wider idea of 'business' people in the CBI-ish sense became important as the world changed more (along with deferential lower-middles and those 'angels in marble' – working-class Tories).[208]

But recently they seem to have been changing much faster and less predictably. And over the last ten years the idea of the party as a 'broad church' with 'wings' and 'interest groups', including subsets of toff-inclined 'one-nation' types restraining the radical suburban right-wingers, has been ditched. Think of Margaret Thatcher and the restraining influence of toff home secretary Willie Whitelaw. One-nation Tories were (modestly) socially liberal and charitable in a noblesse oblige way. But since David Cameron resigned in 2016 they've been thrown out of those gabled windows at a lick, especially after Johnson's 2019 election victory (just listen to what serious one-nation Tories say about the party now).

What's emerged over the period and was shown in surprisingly sharp relief at the last Tory conference is a new billionaire-supported populist approach. It's actually been going on for years. The Conservatives have seriously bought into the Republican playbook. The deep background is the analyses and advice the US right-wing, Koch-funded, 'dark money' think-tanks have been giving – along with very well-paid speaking engagements – to their favourite Tories for years. Policy stuff.

But, more startling, the Tories have now bought the whole 'culture wars' rhetoric that Trump and friends live by. *Listen to what they say.* Start with Suella but listen to the echoes everywhere. Isaac Levido, the Tories in-house campaign director based at No. 4, worked for Sir Lynton Crosby, the Americanised Australian campaigner-for-hire.[209] He has clearly brought in language the Tories' front women and men didn't think up for themselves. The idea of 'luxury beliefs' aired by Suella, for instance, implies that there is an obvious financial hierarchy in the beliefs you can afford. Human rights, from the Act of 1998, which includes such luxurious demands as article 2, 'Right to life", or article 3, 'Prohibition of torture' or 4 'Prohibition of slavery and forced labour' is labelled by Suella as "The Criminal Rights Act" and only for rich poshos.

The close instructive connection between the Tory right and US MAGA-land was something that Johnson as PM was understandably unwilling to acknowledge; he knew it didn't play well with the majority of Brits of *all* parties (privately, of course, he seemed decidedly close to Steve Bannon and Donald Trump and announced in the *Daily Mail* on 19 January 2024 that he was backing Trump as US president).[210] But it became clear from the top and centre of the party, meaning Prime Minister Sunak, that Nigel Farage, bane of several earlier Tory PMs' lives and opening act at a number of Trump MAGA rallies (he left the Tories in 1992) would be welcome back in Tory-land.[211] Farage very publicly said no to the offer. Now the Tories have lost this election and Farage's mates are likely to take over – they include Jacob Rees-Mogg and Liz Truss – then it might be a different answer. And a very different party. Would they still hang out in that gabled imperial pastiche. And how would they do at attracting those big donors?

The Rest is behind the bins

Martin Rowson 23

Door 2
55 Tufton Street

No. 55 Tufton Street is the home of a shifting cast of (nine or so) right-wing think tanks, some of them tenants since it was set up in 2010, some of them newer, brought into life to fight a particular cause and then fade away. The best known, longest-standing, most popular, out-there Tufton Street organisation is the TaxPayers' Alliance (TPA), invented in 2004 by marvellous Matthew Elliott,[212] the co-creator and co-organiser of the whole house-full of organisations, the former CEO of Vote Leave and a founding member of Conservative Friends of Russia (since disbanded).

The TPA, plus other organisations including the Global Warming Policy Foundation, Civitas, the New Culture Forum, European Foundation, Feeding Britain, Global Vision, LGB Alliance and Migration Watch UK appear to be separate but they're not remotely like, say, the different corporate tenants of different floors of a big office block in Victoria Street round the corner. They're much more chummy than that, much more united in ideology and strategy with an interwoven cast of employees who all sort-of relate to Mr Elliott in one way or another.

According to Shahmir Sanni, a former employee of Vote Leave and of the TaxPayers' Alliance, they are differently 'branded' expressions of a common ideology and intent – extreme libertarian free-market warriors who act as one when it really matters. They are all for a small state, low-tax, low-regulation world (and for 'freedom' of a kind they define differently at different times).

They are against publicly funded universal provision organisations like the NHS and the BBC (knowing that these aren't always popular views, they tend to say that they're inefficient or outdated or populated by mad Marxists rather than that they're opposed to them in principle). They'd rather that these things were organised more like they are in America.

They're all against climate change orthodoxy and zero-carbon restrictions too. Another of the longest-standing tenants, the Global Warming Policy Foundation, has that brief. If Tufton Street tenants moved as one, coordinating themes and media schedules, as Shahmir Sanni claimed, they were also coordinated with the local network of longer-standing right-wing think tanks. These were the people next door, up the road and round the corner in attractive Georgian and mock-Georgian houses that strike innocent American tourists as traditionally British (whereas they actually contain organisations more like Washington's legendary K Street, stacked with mega-money lobbyists, than anywhere else in the world).

The reason thoughtful people talk about the generation of post-war right-wing UK think tanks, starting with the Institute of Economic Affairs – old friends of the 55ers who are just round the corner in Lord North Street – in inverted commas is because there's a question of affiliations. The earlier think tanks invited comparison with 'real' academics in 'real' learned organisations or between-wars organisations like the Brookings Institute or the Ford Foundation who employ armies of real researchers doing real things, but they were actually *very* different. The IEA (est. 1955) and its local, different friends certainly did research of a kind and issued reports and involved people with rather academic-sounding titles like 'fellow' but they were characterised from the start by being *much* more clearly partisan and *much more media driven* than traditional academics. They got their reports into friendly papers and their spokespeople on TV. Over the years the BBC has platformed many of these vocal people, especially the IEA's, *without explaining who they really were to viewers or listeners*. All this earlier generation of think tanks had a 'dignified' way of presenting themselves – Old Westminster style. And, though chummy, they didn't all live in the same boarding house (whereas London wags like to joke about the Tufton Street tenants being driven mad by overcrowding in the offices upstairs).

By contrast, 55 Tufton Street, is full of 21st-century, Americanised organisations, driven by street-fighting Leavers who like getting out there congratulating each other on YouTube. One of them – the New Culture Forum,[213] fronted by Peter Whittle, the former UKIP London mayoral candidate – runs a constant series of YouTube panel discussions where all the speakers invoke against liberal elites, cancel culture and the woke mob generally, which might just make an accidental viewer from Rotherham wonder who exactly they were talking about.

The LGB Alliance (see Chapter 12), are newcomers to No. 55, and seem somewhat out of place. They were founded by two mature lesbians, Bev Jackson and Kate Harris, veterans of the 70s gay liberation movement. Its mission is ostensibly support for gays in all ways. But in practice they seem wildly anti-trans. And that's why they're there.

Door 3
2 Lord North Street

The Institute of Economic Affairs, based at 2 Lord North Street (named after Lord North, PM from 1770 to 1782) is on the corner of Great Peter Street, and has elevations to the two streets. The first, undoubtedly original, side is early 18th-century blackened brick with several secretive-looking bricked-up windows – a response to the Window Tax of 1696. The other, Lord North St side was rebuilt around 1907, according to Pevsner (though it looks identical).

Like so many organisations in its London political world, the IEA is clothed in the architectural cover of an early 18th-century terrace. The kind of thing that gets conservative fogeys like the late Sir Roger Scruton pink with pleasure at the absolute *rightness* and modest Englishness of it all.

It's deceptive because the IEA is actually the *global* grandaddy of opaquely funded right-wing think-tankery, a post-war invention taken up at scale by American billionaires. It's closer to the 'political technology' taught in Russian universities than anything in Olde Blighty. The IEA's most prized connection with a prime minister wasn't with Lord North, but with the short lettuce term of Liz Truss, a prized pupil, who apparently spoke at more IEA events than any other politician in the last 12 years.[214] When Truss was elected there were high hopes in Lord North Street that she'd carry out their instructions as set out in their policy reports – and God knows she tried! These reports inevitably recommended a smaller state/lower taxes and less regulation. They said it'd lead to growth.

The IEA's various anonymous donors – they're very secretive about their names – share a passionate dislike of regulation.

Think tanks like the IEA are often called 'libertarian', and say they're keen on 'freedom', meaning the freedom for, say, non-dom billionaires to do their stuff unrestricted. These think tanks provide governments – overwhelmingly right-wing ones – with ready-made policies and, often, ready-made people to help them execute them, either as recruits or 'consultants'. They also think up arguments and buzzwords for politicians to spout. Things they couldn't have invented themselves, let alone argued through. Look across the world and you see the IEA's peers telling the world's Suella Bravermans how to shut up protestors they don't like – from Just Stop Oil to Help Palestine. Their idea of freedom is *very* selective.

The IEA was co-founded in 1955 by Antony Fisher and Oliver Smedley. Fisher was an Etonian battery chicken-farming millionaire pioneer from a wealthy mining family. He was keen to reverse the changes brought in by the Labour government of 1945. He was also a worshipper of Friedrich Hayek, godfather of libertarian philosophy, then at the LSE, who told the young Fisher he should be an *influencer* rather than a party politician.

From the start the IEA led with the gravitas of an impressively bland name and a quasi-academic style (though its reporting wasn't impartial or peer reviewed). In Chapter 1 we saw the revealing letter Smedley wrote to Fisher in 1955 that they must be 'cagey' about what they really wanted in their manifesto.

The IEA created an international model for right-wing think tanks. When Fisher met the fossil fuel multi-billionaire American Koch brothers in the US in the 1970s, he inspired them to create – along with a raft of other billionaires, including a Mellon banking heir – the hugely funded structures of modern American think-tankery. These included the Heritage Foundation, the Cato Institute and the Institute for American Prosperity. They took Fisher's ideas on in an American way at a far greater scale, more proactively and more visibly. Out of it came far greater transatlantic cooperation and co-funding of right-wing initiatives – Republican wonks working with their Conservative counterparts, *making right-wing Britain more like the US.*

Eventually, it led to Fisher founding the Atlas Network in 1981.[215] The Atlas Network now links *hundreds* of right-wing, opaquely funded think tanks across the world. It's worked with about 500 establishments in nearly 100 countries. They're US linked, they're trained, networked and financially supported organisations employing broadly the same approaches *from Britain to Brazil.* That's why the IEA's smallish building with its smallish staff of around 30 people is so deceptive.

Until recently the IEA kept a lowish profile working to influence Conservative politicians and sympathetic media, particularly SMET, who often ran with their ideas in huge dramatic spreads. They also got their spokespeople out and about in broadcast media. The BBC, to their eternal shame, have platformed the IEA's spokespeople for decades without explaining to their audiences who they really were and who was funding their arguments.[216]

The Conservative victory of 2019 and then the Liz Truss premiership brought the IEA out in unfamiliar *Sun*-like self-congratulation, 'it was us wot done it'. Now the Tory future is looking so ominous they might just want to paddle back.

MILLBANK TOWER

Door 4
21–24 Millbank

The Henry Jackson Society lives in Millbank Tower, 21–24 Millbank, a very tall tower built in 1963 and designed by Ronald Ward and Partners. It was, for a year after its completion, the tallest building in the UK, until it was beaten by the BT Tower. It's quite well liked, with rather curvy elevations, a generous podium and an Embankment setting. Pevsner describes it as follows: "Ronald Ward & Partners' elegantly shaped Millbank Tower with its irregular shaped forebuilding", "the best office tower in Westminster" and "one of the few office London Towers to have won affection".[217]

It's huge, with lots of tenants, who've notably included a fair few political organisations since it's just up the road from Parliament. It was once home to the Conservative Campaign Headquarters and, in the Nineties, housed Peter Mandelson's Labour Party Comms Unit, which issued rapid responses to media attacks.

The Henry Jackson Society, founded in Cambridge in 2005, is a current tenant, with a smallish staff (of around 18–20 people). Unlike Labour or the 20th-century Tories, the Henry Jackson Society seems *very American*. It's named after Henry Jackson (1912–1983), a 20th-century US Democrat senator who tried to run in the 1976 US presidential election. Jackson was a politician in Washington as a US representative from 1941 and as a senator from 1953 to 1983. He was best known for his committed anti-communism, and he was a key influencer there on a later generation of neo-conservatives. There is a Henry M. Jackson Foundation in the USA, focused on military medicine.

A lot of the issues the UK HJS is concerned with – geopolitical security, terrorism etc – seem to have an America-in-the-world feel. And a lot of people it platforms in its events do too. And people say – it's difficult to be certain because, like a number of Westminster 'right-leaning' think tank organisations, the HJS is opaquely funded – that a number of its donors are probably American too.[218] The HJS guards its donors' names so assiduously that it 'resigned' from the secretariat role for two All-Party Parliamentary Groups (APPGs) on its special subjects of transatlantic and international security and homeland security when new rules on funding disclosure were introduced in 2014[219] rather than reveal their donors. The HJS shares this secretive approach with many of the sympathetic Westminster think tanks down the road.

It's always been described as 'interventionist' in foreign-policy terms – what we'd call 'hawkish'. When it was founded it included a range of members from the centre left to the far right but is seen as having moved ever rightwards and becoming more anti-immigrant and anti-Muslim after it merged with the Centre for Social Cohesion in 2011. Douglas Murray, a high-profile author and international speaker, had joined as associate director in 2011. And the HJS later moved to London, where it became increasingly vocal and influential. Interviewed by the *Jewish Telegraph* in 2016, the HJS's co-founder and executive director Alan Mendoza said: "We work out how to get engaged in politics on a daily basis, *how to influence the media cycle* and how to discuss matters with politicians in a way which has an impact on certain policies".[220]

Some of its earlier, more centrist members left, feeling out of sympathy with the new anti-immigrant etc. strand of its arguments. One American speaker at an HJS event, for instance, said that Muslims have established 'no-go' zones in the UK where they enforce sharia law.[221] That was in 2015. The speaker, Bobby Jindal, then governor of Louisiana, provoked the then London mayor, Boris Johnson, to call his remarks "complete nonsense".[222] It was oddly predictive of the increasing UK belief in the Great Replacement conspiracy theory and of Conservative MP Paul Scully's observations of 26 February 2024 about Sparkhill in Birmingham and Tower Hamlets in London being no-go areas.[223] And Douglas Murray had famously said, back in 2006, "Conditions for Muslims in Europe must be made harder across the board: Europe must look like a less attractive proposition."[224]

It was also oddly predictive of Lee Anderson MP's attacks on the Muslim mayor of London, Sadiq Khan, who he accused on GB News of "giving our capital away to his mates… Islamists have got control of Khan and they've got control of London". And then, on 1 March 2024, Prime Minister Rishi Sunak swept to a lectern outside No. 10 and said something alternately dramatic and gnomic about threats to the country from people who couldn't exactly be named.

It was a rant about the enemies within, who threatened "the world's most successful multi-ethnic, multi-faith democracy": they were, according to Sunak, "Islamic extremists and the far right (who) feed off and embolden each other… when actually those groups are two sides of the same extremist coin".[225]

This made sense on the page, although there was nothing to explain what the far-right references were about. But the "Islamism" was clearly referencing a subset of the Gaza ceasefire protestors. Then Sunak went on to fill out the picture by saying "But no, you cannot call for violent Jihad [or]… beam antisemitic tropes onto Big Ben" and "there can be no cause you can use to justify the support of a proscribed terrorist group like Hamas".

So it was clear what the PM was saying about the protestors, and that he appeared to be introducing the idea of new legislation to restrict protestors in unnamed ways. And clear that the government will also "act to prevent people entering this country whose aim is to undermine our values". So that's the asylum seekers covered. Having sacked Lee Anderson (who defected to Reform UK on 11 March 2024), the government took a sneaky part-possession of his ideas, larded with high-flown sentiments you never found 30p Lee expressing. Some people call this kind of now-you-see-it-now-you-don't statement 'tactical racism'.

Conveniently/predictably/loyally the *Daily Mail* headline the following morning was 'Rishi delivers speech Britain needed to hear'. The article that followed from Quentin Letts, former funny reviewer, now famous for books explaining who has "buggered Britain" (mainly woke/progressive softie lefties, it seems). Letts explained that it was all about Sunak's key line "there are forces here at home trying to tear us apart". The forces were clearly the ceasefire demonstrators (no doubt Sunak's scriptwriters had debated over whether to call them 'dark' forces and thought 'best not').

It sounded as if – even though Sunak conspicuously wouldn't spell it out – he thought the marches were largely populated by Jihadis and were asking for the elimination of Israel. But actual observers often said that the marches included many races and very visible contingents of Jews critical of Israel. They said they were overwhelmingly peaceful (the comparison was with unpeaceful football crowds!).

George Galloway, of course, just after his Rochdale election victory, was, by implication, another strange 'force'. Meaning that the 66% of UK adults who told YouGov in February 2024 that they wanted Israel to stop and call a ceasefire (up from 59% in the November 2023 poll) are at least endorsing those "forces". The weight of actual public opinion barely gets a look-in with this kind of argument. Nor do far-right extremists; attacks on Muslims have tripled since this time last year (antisemitic attacks have apparently increased thirteen times).[226]

There are allegations linking the HJS with the American right, and particularly with the world of Steve Bannon.[227] A key linkman here – literally – is Raheem Kassam, who worked for the HJS as campaigns director in 2011 and in 2014 joined Nigel Farage's team at UKIP and was immortalised riding with Farage in the golden Trump Tower lift up to Donald J. Trump's penthouse in November 2016. They were the first Brits to congratulate him personally. Kassam and Bannon were involved in media conversations and events with the HSJ thereafter. As we've seen already, Steve Bannon pops up constantly in accounts of British right-wing life of the last decade.[228] And European. And American.

Robin Simcox, the current 'Commissioner for Countering Extremism', was in the news in March 2024 saying that pro-Palestinian protests were making London a no-go zone for Jews:

> We have not betrayed democracy if extremists are no longer able to operate television channels.
>
> And we will not have become an authoritarian state if London is no longer permitted to be turned into a no-go zone for Jews every weekend.[229]

Mr Simcox, appointed by Priti Patel, who'd been on the HJS Advisory Council from 2013 to 2016, was, so it turned out, *a former HJS employee*.[230] And a Heritage Foundation associate (a reminder: they're the far-right Washington think tank writing the plan for the next Trump presidency!). In these roles he's given speeches at a number of right-leaning institutions here and in America, and appeared as a 'terrorism expert' on a number of TV and radio programmes. It could provoke people to ask whether there should be a difference between a government specialist in a vital role and a partisan propagandist.

The more you know about the HJS, the more fascinating it becomes, with the questions of where it is driven from and funded and the question of the very significant access and influence with the last Conservative government it appears to have had. Experts point to the merger of the Department for International Development into the Foreign Office in June 2020. This move had been proposed in an HJS report in February 2019. Boris Johnson (then a backbench MP, before becoming prime minister) had spoken at the report's launch event and he endorsed its conclusions. HJS also hosted a private meeting in London in July 2020, between Mike Pompeo, then US secretary of state, Boris Johnson and foreign secretary Dominic Raab to discuss to the isolation of China, and in particular, the exclusion of Chinese companies from UK telecoms etc. infrastructure involvement. The Americans were convinced that the Chinese spied on the West with their components – and, spookily, that they could control us from Bejing. The UK then fell into line.

The ubiquitous (in the Anglosphere at least) influencer/author/ speaker Douglas Murray, fostered into the great world of foreign affairs by HJS, nonetheless doesn't always command universal admiration in high places. In that well-known Marxist journal *Conservative Home*, Andrew Gimson, the biographer of Boris Johnson and the author of *Kings and Queens: Brief Lives of the Forty Monarchs since 1066* (so clearly a subversive), reviewing Murray's *The War on the West* in May 2022, said, "This author makes, in his introduction, a number of preposterous claims". And Gimson finishes by saying "the Ukrainians' fight for freedom reminds us how trivial most of the pseudo-war recounted in this book really is".[231]

Daily Mail

NORTHCLIFFE HOUSE

GRRRRRRRRRRRrr!!!

Door 5
2 Derry Street

Northcliffe House on Derry Street, Kensington, lives inside the shell of Barker's department store building which faces on to Kensington High Street. The architect of this late High Deco building, Bernard George, designed it in 1937/8 – and it completely looks the part with its bronzed window frames and assertive square tower. However, it was only completed in 1958, long after Deco was replaced by mass Modernism, and long before the Deco architectural revival of the 70s and 80s. *So aesthetically and culturally a bit out of its time.*

In the 1980s an extraordinary conversion was effected from department store to office block. Opening from the side/Derry Street entrance, an impressive 80s US/City-style atrium was constructed with escalators and soaring ceilings which impressed early goggle-eyed visitors to the headquarters of the *Daily Mail* and General Trust, Associated Newspapers and a variety of other enterprises/brands, owned by a PLC then headed by the 3rd Viscount Rothermere, Vere Harmsworth. It is now a private company – with the 4th Viscount, Jonathan Harmsworth, as chairman and controlling shareholder.[232] The business is a conglomerate of – broadly – media businesses, but a fair bit besides.

The *Daily Mail* is the UK's bestselling print newspaper in a market of declining print sales and advertising. Its online incarnation, Mail Online – an international success – is very different from the older traditional broad middle-class brand persona of its parent. Mail Online is famous for photographs of celebrities in bikinis.

Viscount Rothermere, although head of a flag-wavingly patriotic organisation, is in fact a 'non-dom' with non-domicile tax status[233] and apparently owns his media business through a complex structure of offshore holdings and trusts. This is not unlike the two other owners who – as I write – along with Rothermere control ownership of something at least like 80%-plus of UK newspapers' print sales: Rupert Murdoch and the surviving Barclay brother Sir Frederick Barclay. Murdoch is said to have paid no UK tax since 1988 and the Barclay brothers established residence on the island of Brecqhou decades ago. This pattern of ownership is likely to be perpetuated whoever ends up owning the Telegraph Group, which is currently contested. It won't be Sheikh Mansour bin Zayed Al-Nahyan, the UAE vice-president, who wanted it. It might very likely be hedge-funder Sir Paul Marshall, currently co-owner of GB News along with the Legatum Group of Dubai, whose New Zealand-born leader Chris Chandler, a former hedge-funder, is understandably assumed to be a non-dom too.

This combination of performative patriotism – flags, wartime references, obsession with the monarchy, anti-multiculturalism, etc. – often seems to go, at the financial top end, with a preference for sunnier tax regimes.

The *Daily Mail* is fiercely against left-wingery of all kinds, especially when practised by anyone remotely approaching the wealth and smartness of their ruling family. The woke mob – a popular locution in *Mail*-land – is said to be populated by people who hold, in Suella Braverman's term, 'luxury beliefs' (see Door 1).

There's more.

The *Mail* calls this sort of thing 'virtue signalling' (a term invented by James Bartholomew in the *Spectator* in 2015).[234] Thirty years ago it would've called beliefs it disliked "political correctness" (gone mad!) and back in the old David English/Linda Lee-Potter days their columnists would've talked about "hypocritical do-gooders".

Back then, in the *Mail*'s demonology, they probably lived in North London, possibly in "town houses" (Suella Braverman again!). If so, they'd have qualified for membership of the *Metropolitan Liberal*

Elite, a vaguely defined group (see Chapter 11) that includes what the *Mail* considers the "enemies of the people" – its famous headline of 4 November 2016, attacking the judges for ruling that the process for leaving the EU would require the consent of Parliament (they noted in passing that one of the judges was 'openly gay'). The 20th-century origins of the "enemies" phrase lie in Stalinist Russia.[235] Khrushchev's repudiation of his predecessor in 1956 explicitly traced it to Stalin.

The *Mail* has a talent for trolling, attacking individuals and groups it doesn't like, for a variety of reasons. It does it most entertainingly. It doesn't like Harry and Megan for instance – Harry is suing them and Meghan just isn't their kind of person. According to them, she's arrogant and self-obsessed whereas, say, the Princess of Wales isn't any of those bad things.

The *Mail* also dislikes senior civil servants who advise against the policies of right-wing Tory governments. These people are, the *Mail* says, "The Lump", part of the "anti-growth coalition" that Liz Truss so deplored. The *Mail* absolutely loved Liz Truss, greeting her epic budget of 24 September 2022 with another of its equally epic headlines, 'At last a real Tory budget'.

The *Mail* loves to hate. Describing the winning formula for his *Daily Mail* in 1914, its popular founder Alfred Harmsworth (1865–1922), later Lord Northcliffe – brother of the then Viscount Rothermere, Jonathan Harmsworth's great-grandfather – famously said "I give my readers a daily hate". They've been at it for some time. It's probably the origin of the Daily Hate ritual in Orwell's *Nineteen Eighty-Four*, published in 1949.

The *Daily Mail*'s hatchet jobs are legendary. Its targets – left-wing politicians, feminists, anti-racism groups or trans-activists are always described in personality and lifestyle terms, and they're revealed to be variously arrogant, unpatriotic, adulterous, comfortably bourgeois, obsessive, gay or even a bit foreign. The *Mail*'s hatchet jobs never engage with its victims' political arguments; *they just do them over*, based on the proven principle that if you discredit the man or woman you discredit their causes.

A 1980s media wag used to say that the *Mail* had a 'rogue debutante desk' back in the day. The idea was that when any rebellious left-leaning protest group emerged – and better still, organised a public protest – the *Mail*'s brilliant deb desk, practised in spotting the children of aristocrats and plutocrats, would bravely direct the photographer to catch the earl's daughter or the A-list pop star's son shouting for women's rights or racial justice. That gave them tomorrow's headline. Young people so insanely privileged as this – people who 'don't know they're born' – back this cause, not respectable suburbanites like you, gentle reader. So you know you shouldn't. It works every time.

Doors 6 & 7
Riverbank House & The Point

You'd expect GB News, the extravagantly flag-draped new right-wing broadcaster launched in July 2021, to be housed in somewhere that looked a bit like a Wetherspoons. But its office headquarters and its studios are both in sleek, shiny non-committal international-looking buildings from the Noughties boom. One is at Riverbank House in Swan Lane EC4 – the City, where the business is registered. The studios are in The Point at 37 North Wharf Road, one off those newish blocks in the Paddington Basin development, completed in 2003, the ones you see on your left after you turn off the Edgware Road towards the flyover. The building was designed by Sir Terry Farrell – him of the exuberant 80s postmodern TV-AM building in Camden Lock with the eggcup roofline and a later cluster of international buildings to rival Sir Norman Foster's.

The idea behind GB News could be argued to come from Dominic Cummings in his infamous blog of 2004 which outlined his plan to destroy the BBC.[236] It had to be done, so he said, because the BBC was the 'mortal enemy' of the Conservative Party, which would never regain power while the BBC existed in its present form. His five-point plan was extraordinarily modern and media savvy by British 2004 standards. Cummings had spent three years in Russa – enough to see how Putin's propaganda strategies worked – and he clearly also followed the US 'political technology' media scene closely.

One crucial part of the Cummings plan was to set up a national TV broadcaster like Fox News, a populist right-wing station, to take viewers from BBC News and undermine its reputation with a livelier, more demotic tabloid approach to TV current affairs. Something altogether less 'liberal elite' which could reflect the public concerns the BBC wouldn't acknowledge – the sort of things you might conceivably hear in Wetherspoons.

Cummings was a pioneer, but it took until 2020 for the investors and the crucial familiar frontman to be put together. The first major investor was US media giant Discovery and then Legatum Ventures Ltd, the Dubai-based finance group run by New Zealand-born hedge-funder Christopher Chandler, who'd apparently made his alleged billion-plus in 'distressed situations' in 1990s Russia.[237] The other key investor was Sir Paul Marshall, a British hedge-fund trader, who, according to the *Sunday Times* Rich List, is estimated to be worth around £630 million. As we've seen, Sir Paul Marshall also owns UnHerd, the online 'eclectic' right-wing site (it's been described as a younger, cooler *Spectator*). And he wants to buy the Telegraph Group – which includes the *Spectator*. There was a successful campaign to stop the government of Abu Dhabi buying the group, presumably so Sir Paul can steam ahead.

That prize GB News frontman was Andrew Neil, formerly the BBC's most senior political presenter, who'd fallen out with the Corporation. Neil is a former editor of the *Sunday Times* and founding chairman of Sky TV, a brilliant interviewer, a heavyweight in every sense. He helped make the GB News project investable and he made the world take it seriously rather than rushing to judgement. However, the first few weeks were inadvertently hilarious: there were wobbly sets and production glitches and some new presenters who'd clearly hadn't done this sort of thing before (and some who seemed – to the viewers brought in by the Andrew Neil promise – distinctly naff). The initial audience of checkers-out fell disastrously after a few days.

According to the hyper-authoritative media analyst Enders Analysis in July 2023: "The two news channels' viewing levels remain niche. Since the launch of TalkTV, the average daily reach of GB News (601,000) and TalkTV (254,000) remains dwarfed by Sky News (1.75 million) and BBC News (2.36 million), though the gap has been narrowing recently. GB News and TalkTV viewers are on average older than those of Sky News and BBC News. While GB News is faring slightly better, it is still dependent on a very small and loyal core of viewers. The heaviest ten percent of GB News viewers make up 73% of the channel's viewer minutes, watching 3.4 hours per week on average. 81% of these heavy viewers are over 55, 56% do no paid work, 57% are male, 90% are white British and 76% left school before the age of 19."[238]

(The gap between GB News, Sky News and the BBC has somewhat narrowed since then, but the rank order hasn't changed, whatever the GBN people say.)

After presenting just eight programmes in three months, Andrew Neil announced that he was leaving. He'd looked completely miserable onscreen from the word go; his body language said he'd realised he'd been slumming it with the GB gang. It wasn't just a question of political sympathies – this was the man who'd introduced the *Sunday Times* audience to neo-conservatism after all – but he didn't want to spend his valuable time in Wetherspoons.

I heard later that Neil – tough as old boots, you'd think – was deeply depressed after he left. He'd made – unusually – a wrong move into a different culture. What he said publicly at first was that the persistent production problems at GB News were the problem. "It was really beginning to affect my health. I wasn't sleeping, I had a constant knot in my stomach." Later he said that he was in a "minority of one: on the board (where he was chairman), and that it had been the worst mistake of his life.[239]

After that, wags pointed to the rapidly declining viewing figures – at one point so low as barely to register on the conventional media trade index BARB. In August 2022, the big mainstream media investor Discovery sold out for £8 million, leaving two hedge-funders with a shared political view owning most of the business. Chandler's Legatum Group had set up the Legatum Institute – in a smart London house – in 2007 as a think tank/pressure group with a vague mission to 'promote prosperity'. It was observed to move very significantly to the right over the following 15+ years. People asked aloud whether GB News was really intended to make any money ever, or was it a purely political project?

One media commentator I talked to raised the simple question of whether GB News (and TalkTV, still going at the time but now closed down) were quite simply the best way you could contribute to the right's electoral fortunes – whether that meant Conservative, Reform or any other right-wing party.[240] If you just gave them what it'd cost to run GB News for a year – call it around £30 million – it'd be a *very* high profile donation, and they'd waste it anyway, because they wouldn't know how to spend it. And in any case there were legal limits on political spending in this country. So it might be far better to get them some 'third-party endorsements' was my informant's thinking.

GB News has stirred constant controversy and constant viewer complaints, leading on to constant Ofcom references. By October 2023, Ofcom had found GB News had breached its licence on six separate occasions – five of them 'significant' and four more investigations were still pending. Significantly Ofcom – described by the veteran TV political journalist Michael Crick as 'one of the weakest institutions on the planet' – hasn't imposed any sanctions yet as a result of these. This meant, in turn, that it would embolden other broadcasters to push the limits. The GBN management said, perhaps humorously, that it would introduce better training!

Three crucial issues have dogged GB News' recent performance. The first and most persistent is its widely alleged role as a Conservative Party mouthpiece. It has a roster of Tory MP presenters talking to each other or to senior Tory minsters – as when the married duo of MPs Esther McVey and Philip Davies interviewed Chancellor Jeremy Hunt in what looked like a positively Soviet set-up. And GB News' most watched presenter is Nigel Farage. This alignment dramatises the significant rightward populist move of the Tory party, where the familiar lines between what used to be called the 'centre right' and the far-right margins seemed to dissolve (in the way prefigured by the playwright David Edgar in his 1976 play *Destiny*).

Everything else is about Dan Wootton. Wootton was GB News' lead presenter before his suspension – he wasn't actually dismissed then – on 27 September 2023. He was suspended for appearing to endorse Laurence Fox's misogynistic 'would-you-shag-her?' remarks about leftish journalist Ava Evans. The suspension was very convenient for GB News; it gave them notional brownie points but, more important, it gave them a relatively comfortable way of getting the embarrassing Wootton off the stage without exposing the viral rumours about him.

As *Byline Times* readers – and a good many more eager online explorers – know, there's a jaw-dropping *Byline Times* story about Wootton by Dan Evans and Tom Latchem that's been circulating for months.[241] But amazingly, *with almost no mainstream media uptake.* (But, to be fair, there has been no police action to date.) This is a combination of a) a sympathetic blackout from right-wing newspapers, b) absolute self-censoring terror of the subject on the part of mainstream broadcasters and c) very tough legal warnings served on absolutely everyone else. So half the country knows and the other half doesn't. Just imagine if anything like this had emerged about any other remotely visible media figure. Just think about the coverage of the Philip Schofield or Huw Edwards stories, which, without going back into the familiar details, *don't even come close*. It tells you a lot about 'press freedom'.

We know that Sir Paul Marshall, hedge-funder and co-owner of GB News, is widely reported as an eager bidder for the Telegraph Group[242] – which could make him the Conservative kingmaker to replace Rupert Murdoch. He must be very keen that GB News should be seen to keep a tidy house. And Dan Wootton *was* quietly dismissed by GB News on 5 March 2024.

Metropolitan Illiberal Elites

I live in Westminster between two tremendously topical elite territories. Just up the road, cut off by the train tracks from Victoria, is Belgravia, positively festering with all the remaining Russian oligarchs behind Cubitt's 1830s cream stucco. To the other side, past the Vauxhall Bridge Road and pushing on towards Parliament Square, there's another powerful elite group, tightly clustered, highly secretive about its workings and finances, held together by aligned interests and a sort of informational/propaganda food chain. It's a very professional and focused world, yet one animated by the romance of political Westminster and a weird sense of victimhood. And the joy of winning.

This world is made up of lobbyists, right-wing think-tankers and pressure groups, political editors from right-wing newspapers and some of their favourite columnists, certain Conservative MPs and their parliamentary SPADs (let's call them Tory boyz). They're linked to real power; they're the connective tissue. They connect to central government, to real decision-takers and, in a more shadowy way, to all the people who pay for this influencing.

There are the lobbyists' clients – the opaquely funded think tanks' big secret donors. There are big corporations. There are big money individuals – hedge-funders and big private companies. And the money comes from here and from there – from fundraising arms in America, from US 'foundations' that share their aims. Even, according to some people recently, from Russia.

And as we've seen, at 55 Tufton Street SW1 there's a shifting population of small think tanks and pressure groups all founded this century and shepherded into coordination by Matthew Elliott, the former CEO of Vote Leave, inventor of the TaxPayers' Alliance in 2004. Round the corner in attractive 18th-century Lord North Street is the Institute of Economic Affairs, role model to hundreds of similar organisations across the Anglosphere and wider.

At 111 Buckingham Palace Road, there's the Telegraph Media Group, until recently owned by the surviving Barclay brother and, in an attractive street to the other, St James's side of Victoria Street, there's the 191-year-old *Spectator* magazine also recently owned by Frederick Barclay and edited from 1999 to 2005 by Boris Johnson.

The *Spectator's* former political editor was James Forsyth, married to Allegra Stratton, the one victim of Partygate and the former press secretary to the government. Rishi Sunak was Forsyth's best man and a great friend from Winchester. Now Forsyth works for Sunak as his political secretary.

At 11 Tufton Street is Public First – the research/PR/lobbying firm owned by James Frayne, friend and one-time business partner of Dominic Cummings from the early 2000s. Frayne's wife and current business partner is Rachel Wolf, who co-wrote the previous Conservative Party manifesto with Munira Mirza – Boris Johnson's long-standing supporter as London's deputy mayor for culture and then, until recently, director of the No. 10 Policy Unit. The other co-author was Robert Colvile, director of one of the Conservatives' favourite think tanks, the Centre for Policy Studies.

Are you beginning to get the picture of all the talent and cooperation jammed into this little network of old streets behind Victoria Street, clustered around Westminster School and Parliament? But what should we call this secret dedicated band of brothers and sisters? The metropolitan illiberal elite is the powerful group that's forever perpetuating the right-wing meme of the metropolitan *liberal* elite – that annoying, woke, high-minded group who, in right-wing newspapers and magazines, *is said to run the world.*

Are you, or have you ever been, a member of the metropolitan liberal elite? Ask yourself whether you've ever even vaguely favoured a 'liberal' cause. Or whether you've ever lived in a London postal district, particularly NW3, NW1 or N1. Maybe you've attended a middle-class dinner party in one of those areas. Or worked in the 'creative industries', particularly public service broadcasting (ITV, C4, C5, above all the BBC). Then you'll do.

Like those judges in the *Daily Mail* – well paid, well educated – you're obviously on your way to being an Enemy of the People. To hear right-wing newspapers – remember, more than 80% of print sales by UK national newspapers are broadly 'right'; they're the ones owned by tax-exile billionaires – you'd think these MLEs were actually in charge of everything. You'd think they had all the power and all the money. After all, some of those liberal creative types – star actors and directors – do very nicely.

But do they actually run the government? Do they run the City? Do they run the world's largest global corporations? Are they actually billionaires? Do they work in politics all day long?

Get a grip.

So let's meet the various personality types of the Illiberal Elite – the fairground mirror images of the woke mob, eco-zealots, trans-activists and the rest.

1 The Fogey Historian

The Fogey Historian can always be relied on for a dose of Victorian Values. He'll come out fighting the in the *Telegraph* when any great institution gets a bit hand-wringing about, say, its links to slavery. He says it's nothing to do with their core purpose of scholarship or conservation and they shouldn't give in to the woke mob.

He is stubby and tubby, forever in elaborate three-piece tweed suit. Even his waistcoats have waistcoats. Some of his 19th-century enthusiasms – particularly those strong men of Empire – get liberals hot under the collar now and he absolutely loves it that way.

It all adds up to his currency as a pukka academic who's not afraid to be hard hitting in defence of Traditional Britain. Some naïve types, clocking the dress code and the period enthusiasms, assume that he's gay. They couldn't be more wrong (his wife – the third – had reckoned that too, before she first got into a taxi with him).

2 @TheToryBoyz

Their friends call them Bill and Ben – actually they're Robert and William – for their odd similarity. Their constant blue-suited formality is just like those Westminster boy estate agents'. They don't dress like their contemporaries – they're 27 and 28 – you *never* see them in trainers or denim, though they're always being asked to provide 'the perspective of your generation' at the constant policy wonk conferences they go to, supporting and clevering-up their bosses. Until recently, Robert worked for a notable right-wing Tory junior minister, making sure he's briefed about practically everything, writing his speeches and helping him avoid dangerous gaffes, particularly when he's had a few.

William works in a think tank in a nice Georgian house round the corner, producing policy reports that the national newspapers and magazines love. They prove beyond doubt that, say, well-meaning 'progressive' policies actually disadvantage minority groups in the workplace. Or that naïve over-regulation from The Blob (traditional civil servants), stops 'levelling-up' by intimidating young red wall entrepreneurs in the making.

They live together in their clever little former council flat snuggled conveniently behind the Tate. They're an item. They don't hide it, or make a thing of it; it's factored in. It's as if their teen and early twenties life had never happened; they'd been too busy, stacking up the qualifications (good first degrees, PhDs and special training in special places like George Mason University in Fairfax County, Virginia). They were born old.

3 Are You Thinking What She's Thinking?

Now Katie Hopkins is pretty much off the stage, there's a vacancy for the top middle-middle-class, middle-aged angry voice of the nicer Home County suburbs. The precedent was set in print – in the *Mail* and the *Express*, with women like Linda Lee-Potter. Later iterations, like the *Mail*'s Jan Moir, had to up the ante ("Are you thinking what she's thinking?") for a less inhibited audience. Sarah Vine kept things going (she knows you know!), and Amanda Platell added a sharp colonial note. And Katie Hopkins, with her compelling mix of suburban Sloane snobbery and out-there prejudices, practically broke the mould.

Cathy's a leading contender now because she's good on TV, and quick on radio. She's just lawyer's-wife-RP enough without being annoyingly posh. And just presentable enough without being annoyingly young and glam! And now she's got a big TV job. Cathy's written across the circuit – *Telegraph*, *Mail* and *Express*. She's totally reliable; they don't have to brief her. She knows what's required. She has a number of specialist subjects, the trans issue being at the top now. Trans, for her, is a subset of the woke mob she sees behind every protest movement, whether it's LGBT, Black Lives Matter or environmentalists (she particularly savours her own description of Extinction Rebellion protesters that she first paraded on a BBC discussion "purring back to Bath in their top-of-the-range Teslas"). Whatever the merits of any of these causes, she always says their followers are all middle-class hypocrites – or, to use the *Spectator* term she's adopted recently, they're all 'virtue signalling'. From time to time when she and her various Cambridge contemporaries get together – they're all early 50s-ish now, and many of them writers. They discuss their political differences, and what the most heartfelt differences between right- and left-wing columnists are now. Cathy, who was mildly but acceptably left at Cambridge, thinks privately it's about £250,000 a year.

4 Illiberal Kerry

Kerry always says she's "of the left". It's difficult to see how exactly she reckons that, given that all her friends are drawn from the right now; all the platforms – physical and media – she mounts are right-wing ones. And all her donors and sponsors and discreet supporters come from the right, here and in the US (lots of American 'foundations' and 'institutes'). Quite far to the right actually. And, above all, the targets she attacks in her frequent speeches, writings and media appearances are always implicitly or explicitly left-wing ones (she's not that bothered about the distinction between centre left and Corbynists either, but given a choice, she hates the centrists more).

She's against the woke as well, whoever they're supposed to be. She says they're against every sort of freedom. This would make her a sort of libertarian (but she doesn't really like that handle either).

When, an age ago, she was a declared far leftist, nonetheless other far leftists with different badges wondered who exactly she hated most – the wicked global imperialists or them. Her taste in campaigns seemed so... *perverse*. Like her curious cohort of comrades who've *usually moved* with her to the fiery furnace of the New Right, where Tory headbangers meet people from an altogether cleverer more global, professional group who tell the Brits how to strategise for the Great Reckoning to come. In the meantime, she's sitting pretty, as one of the right's favourite token minorities.

President-for-Life Lopez
Correctional Plantation
(formerly the Robert Estate)
TWINNED WITH
MARALAGO

FOX NEWS

Wenceslas
INSTITUTE
of
BLOOD
&
SOIL

EUROPEAN
BREXIT
FOUNDATION
for
Selective
Democracy

CENTRE
FOR
WHITE
STUDIES

5 Sloane and Colonial

Robert is what wags call 'Sloane and colonial'. Someone with all the trad right-wing Tory beliefs, styles and semantics, *but so much more so*, meaning he comes across as an English gent as imagined by the Mar-a-Lago crowd. They say it's because he was brought up in a former British colony then packed off to a upper-middling public school before Oxford, where he became increasingly fierce about immigration and the EU. At the same time he became increasingly soft on the Oxbridge romance, particularly *Brideshead*; he often said his ideal home would look like the Radcliffe Camera (and his ideal boy would look like Sebastian Flyte).

Robert is a citizen of the world – never more at home than in a well-funded US institute's conference in Arizona, telling the shocked audience that Britain is in current danger of turning Marxist. He says that within five years there'll be a majority Muslim population with sharia law here too. Basically he's selling the Great Replacement conspiracy theory but in a smarter-sounding way. His inner world is the one of roughly 100 years ago, while most of his English right-wing friends are only 50 years behind.

Some of them wonder, behind his back, how exactly all this travelling is financed. Can these speaking-and-telly tours (Fox and lookalike stations love him) really pay that well? He's always on the go, in the Anglosphere and beyond: Vancouver, Vienna, Versailles. Now he's no longer an MP, the world's his lobster. And the globally linked institutes and foundations pick up the tab.

The concerns of the further right come naturally to him; they're not consciously retro/late-80s Oxford poses. Unlike most of his circle they're what he grew up with. His father, who he always described as "to the right of Attila the Hun" had stayed on in the former colony for profitable decades as an advisor to the showman president-for-life dictator who'd replaced the British. They got on terribly well.

©Martin Rowson 22

6 The Link Man

Jeff is a lot of fun. He has strong beliefs, but he never really says anything about them that his peers don't. And he seems indiscreet, but he never tells you anything that's really surprising or potentially libellous, particularly about the people he sometimes describes as 'assets'. The one thing determinedly, demonstrably special about this affable, well-tailored American-in-London is his range of contacts on either side of the Atlantic (and way further afield), the order of money they seem to have – money's no problem – and the speed at which he can deploy them.

If, for instance you'd written an amazing new book that described the funding of Antifa and its various front organisations and secret workings and you didn't think your publisher was doing much for you, a word from Jeff would change everything. That very week you'd find yourself in say, 5 Hertford Street, for what seemed like a great night out but involves accidentally bumping into Jeff's great friend from Arizona, who links through to a speaking tour and some very nice venues. You'd meet some of the people and institutions that'd helped other Brits such as Liz Truss discussing deregulation in Washington when she was a treasury minister in 2018 and a trade one in 2019. Done: just like that. It's a sort of real-life Atlantic bridge (though strictly not to be confused with the charity/think tank of that name which involved Liam Fox's great friend and travelling companion Adam Werrity. Atlantic Bridge received a lot of critical coverage in 2007 and has since been wound up). You wouldn't associate Jeff, with his nice clipped beard and his perfect Old South manners and his feeling of private money, with more abrasive types such as Donald Trump or Steve Bannon. Or Roger Stone. You assume he's part of a Bush-ite neocon world, well before the Tea Party even. But he's moved with the times; he knows everyone. He knows what's going on at the latest CPAC; Victor Orbán's talking to them next. (Jeff says you should ignore the newspaper stories and that "Victor is a great guy".)

What exactly does he do? He's on boards and advisory committees rather than working as a definable jobsworth anywhere. Most notably, he's connected to an American-international lobbyist/PR company headquartered in K Street, Washington. He's been, as it turns out, a great supporter of Brexit and then a great campaigner for Boris Johnson as UK prime minister. "My British friends think Trump is a ghastly vulgarian," Jeff says "but he's given ordinary Americans their confidence back – and Boris Johnson resembles him more than you think." Alas, Jeff is leaving London soon to work in Paris, whatever that means, leaving just a discreet whiff of Truefitt & Hill Sandalwood. His work here is done.

7 Tracey

Tracey looks mid-to-late 20s – she's actually 32 – and her style is really quite inclusive. Meaning she's British born, mixed race, but no one's quite sure what the elements are. Sometimes she's referred to as a person of colour, sometimes not. And her accent's somewhat Estuarine, but it changes according to the group or the media platform she's talking to. Sometimes she's very Tracey-from-the-block, other times more junior sociology lecturer. And her precise calling slithers about a bit too according to the situation. Sometimes she's a "young activist", sometimes "social commentator", whatever either might actually be.

Her job is to be 'Conservative youth' and her message, whether to students or OAP Ukippers, is that youth often is Conservative, and all those media lefties (our friends in the metropolitan liberal elite) are constantly pretending that they're all rebellious woke students.

Tracey argues against wokeness as something foisted on ordinary modern, ambitious young people. And especially on students, where the foisters are leftie academics, who are absolutely everywhere now according to Tracey. Depending on the audience she will or won't employ the lovely meme 'cultural Marxists', who are pretty much the same as the woke mob, but likely to be more academic.

Tracey is highly trained; she's been on the course, the training which helps her to respond to every situation and every audience. She knows how to get the oldies scandalised on behalf of their grandchildren who are in such danger of being done over by Commies, and she knows how to make a room full of middle-class students feel they don't know a thing about the other 50%-plus of their generation. Or working-class life in general.

Tracey herself could reasonably be described as lower-middle, but upward bound. She's a graduate, though she doesn't always admit it – from somewhere distinctly non-smart. And she spent six years working in at a multinational, while being what Ben Elton called "a little bit political" in her spare time. She leant towards the call of the alt-right. So she was on the radar. And when the call came – basically to become a member of a most unusual 'speaker bureau' – she was ready.

The boot camp training was very American, but Tracey's used to that. And a lot of the people involved in this organisation, which is often a bit shy about itself – meaning Tracey usually isn't 'badged' as coming from them – are either distinctly posh, from several generations of money, or American. All of which is fine by Tracey, who feels she's getting somewhere.

Like her peers from the Special Speaker Bureau, Tracey positively glows when she's introduced on TV discussion programmes. She's immaculate and smiley – it's always been important to her – and so are the boys with their short hair and smart clothes, like nicely dressed young people from a sort of Alternative Love Island.

8 The Soul of Discretion

X likes to see himself as 'X' used to keep score – personally and for the think tank he runs – by the number of their policy briefs the government took up and put into action. Being behind new manifesto promises and legislation was a quiet satisfaction. Recognised by Westminster insiders rather than by *Daily Mail* headlines (it was the Foundation wot done it). The people who needed to know always did, and they mostly kept the trail quiet – the trail that led from anonymous donors with sometimes quite staggering money to spend on 'research' (X privately described it as "case building" while their critics simply called it "lobbying" and latterly "dark money lobbying" after Jane Mayer's book).

X seems as far from his high-profile, big set-up American counterparts as you could imagine. He knows the form, he's as upper-middle-diplomatic as you could imagine and he never says anything remotely extreme sounding or non-PC in public. And he's toned his voice down over the past 15 years so he doesn't come across as any kind of Cameron-style 'posh boy' (in Nadine Dorries-speak). He is quite posh really. And he knows that boasting that two lines in the legislation he's got in the book has saved his 'donor' (read client) literally billions is dangerous.

Worryingly, after 2019, he noticed some of his Westminster think tank peers getting what he'd see as unwelcome attention recently for letting on that they'd been training up key politicians for years. They made it sound all very *Manchurian Candidate*. Others were saying to anyone who'd listen that, behind the scenes, they'd packed the last government with their disturbingly bright-eyed boys and girls, untroubled by doubt. X had put some of his own in there too, but he'd drilled everyone concerned strictly not to be triumphalist. The point of the whole right-wing think tank success has been discretion, persuasion. They're in the business of creating long-term 'assets' by converting people to a Brit-libertarian view, making the whole thing very seductively understated, and a bit high-table academic too with the apparatus of reports and research with 'fellows' and other resonant, clever-sounding job titles.

There are other think tanks in X's world – just up the road in deep Westminster actually – who do a lot with the media. They turn out position papers on, say, 'identity politics' that can make a newspaper's double-page attack spread on the alleged mad Marxists behind Black Lives Matter or Stonewall look like something considered or informed. They've got the time to do the research and grub up the impressive-sounding statistics that the quick turnaround journalists don't have.

That "tabloid fig-leaf stuff", as he calls it, isn't X's mission. They do it sometimes when they've got a big report out, but he believes working with people who've got real power – or will achieve it shortly with his help – makes much more sense. He completely saw the logic of the Brexit campaign as a way of 'reframing' the UK's political conflicts. And he completely saw the point of the red wall initiative. And, of course, he's completely mastered the language. But does he really want to spend much time with these people – some of whom he describes to a few close discreet friends as "attention-seeking inadequates" or, worse still, "suburban psychopaths"?

9 Lord Whitstable Bigging It Up

Lord Whitstable is a big man in every way. Tall, wide and hugely rich. Like so many of the crucial backers of the 2019 Boris Johnson Conservative Party, it's all his own money. It's based in private companies headquartered in a variety of jurisdictions, rather than those boring mainstream corporate businesses. Because he's a proper old-fashioned plutocrat and a king in his own realm, he's free to big it up in the political world. He's one of the super-rich team that then DCMS Secretary of State Nadine Dorries told a bemused Beth Rigby of Sky News in a central lobby interview back in the days were "the big donors who gave the party £80 million last time. They aren't going to support it without Boris Johnson as leader".

The implication back then was that Boris's critics had better shut up or they'd all be sleeping in the gutter. A fair few of Boris's men – they were all men – became Truss's men, like Lord Whitstable, stumping up the estimated £450,000 for her brief leadership campaign in the hope of her long premiership becoming a positive bonfire of the taxes and regulations that so unfairly affected them and their friends.

Lord Whitstable was involved in a number of discreet and delicious dinners presenting the fair and fragrant Liz Truss to the Great and Loaded. Many of this band of brothers were in turn at the famous Chelsea party on the evening of the mini-budget day on 23 September 2022, where guests pressed Kwasi Kwarteng to do more of the same. Lord Whitstable seems to spend a fortune on philanthropy and political influence. Despite all the money he doles out, amazingly he keeps getting richer. His deals – so well-informed you'd think he was telepathic – are really spot on. Like his hedge fund friends, who he likes for their "buccaneering" energy and "sense of humour", he knows when to buy and sell. He buys and sells companies that don't seem to know what they've got. His hedge fund friends buy and sell abstractions and make clever bets on the pound of the heads-I-win-tails-you-lose variety (many did rather well out of the mini-budget!).

Boris Johnson said "Fuck business" and Lord Whitstable agrees. His gang are nothing like the poor wage slave CEOs of the UK corporate sector, cautious to the max, always saying the careful right thing and anxiously looking out for shareholder and pressure group challenges. And all that for just five or six million a year?

Like your average really rich person, Lord Whitstable has more and bigger houses in more exotic places than the rest of us. But because he's crossed the line into 'serious money', which is now really set at the billionaire level, he can buy so much more than just things – he can buy people. He can walk very tall indeed knowing that, in most London rooms, he could buy everyone there. When Boris described his £275,000-a-year deal with the *Telegraph* as "chicken feed" (actually it would put him well within the top 1% of UK income earners) it showed that he'd spent too much time around people like Lord Whitstable. They make him feel very poor. But sadly Lord Whitstable's own 'reference group' makes him feel like an also-ran in the world stakes. He follows American politics eagerly but he's acutely aware that you need, at the very least, $10 billion to walk tall and throw your political weight around there.

10 The Earl of Identity Politics

Hugh or, to give him his full name, Hugh Darnley-Norman (otherwise, for people who know and care deeply about these things, the 14th Earl of X – a full-on belted earl), finds some of his fellow travellers on the New Right quite hard going. Their shoes and their pronunciations in particular. He'd never say anything, of course, but when the noove-plutocrats or the slick 'comms' types talk about "aristocrats like yourself", pronouncing it 'wrist', there's an inner wince. And as for their orange-tan shoes with blue trousers... The Earl of X is much happier with more salt of the Earth types such as Tommy Robinson, whom he greatly admires, or the more blokey old Ukippers who remind him of people who've worked for him.

Like other toffs who've turned from their natural home in the Conservative Party to the far right – now a combination of the people who've always been there and the big-money, American-inspired latecomers – a number of factors are in play. Europe, for a start. Hugh's been seriously 'Eurosceptic' forever and that's pulled him south politically this century because so many of his fellow upper Tories weren't. And he's become increasingly religious in a slightly OTT way as he's got older and things have gone wrong. He's a great one for the Billy Graham Foundation, which he thinks has "many of the right ideas". This hugely amuses old friends in Chelsea, who called him Fun Boy Four, after the noted musical ensemble Fun Boy Three back in the early 80s. It's led to him denouncing the woke mob who he says "rule our media and universities" (the Earl of X didn't go to one – he went into the army).

Then there's the second wife, "the high society model" as the tabloids called her (she'd got her own money), who left him for a very social black entrepreneur with dreadlocks. And the money troubles from some of his more eccentric investments. He's also a great admirer of Turning Point UK, an offshoot of the ultra-right-wing Turning Point US, launched at the RAC in Pall Mall in December 2018 to a smart audience to do battle with wokery, cultural Marxism, cancel culture and other baleful influences apparently threatening the nation's finest young minds in universities.

His children think he's nuts – they wish he'd concentrate on rebuilding their inheritances instead of banging on against Black Lives Matter. "All lives matter, including white ones," he says, and "LGBTQ plus whatever initials it is today" on platforms with a lot of weirdos. They just want a decent house in Chelsea each. Like Dad's. Between the wars, the great houses of Mayfair and Belgravia had a fair few toffs who admired Hitler and Mussolini and what they'd done for their countries – principally, save them from communism. Hitler and Mussolini, both of them distinctly below the salt in origins and style, nonetheless inspired smart girls such as Unity Mitford, the sister of Nancy and Debo, to extreme passion. The Duke of Windsor was well in with the Führer too, but after the war – when former admirers had died fighting for the Allies – fascinating fascism became a taboo subject, and right-leaning toffs were at great pains to explain, like the Earl of X now, they weren't remotely racist or antisemitic. They leave that to Kanye West. In his darkest hours, the Earl of X secretly envies the actor Tim Bentinck, otherwise David Archer from Radio 4 or otherwise the Earl of Portland (created 1689), who seems to have got away from it all scot free.

11 Killer Queen

Craig has invested more than £50,000 in his teeth, well before the pandemic, well before he was appearing on TV regularly. Every visible tooth has been filed down and covered in an iridescent white veneer making the whole set larger, longer, whiter and more uniform. You can't miss them. Some of his friends make jokes about them, but he toughs it out, killer queen-style. It's the price of being in business he says. Every few months he gets needles stuck in various parts of his face – he's only 35 – to no obvious effect. He got these ideas from his role model, Simon Cowell.

Craig follows US media-land avidly, hoping one day to join his idols on, say, Fox. But for the meantime, he's a UK journalist who does politics and showbiz (or rather politics as showbiz) and he's getting more TV work, as stand-in presenter on the new circuit and 'guest' on a number of discussions. When he's on the new circuit he knows he's got lots of competition, some of them ten years younger, from his peers in the gay alt-right/alt-light brigade – the people who tell you the left can't expect their vote, any more than it can expect those of, say, aspirant Asians or black people.

Gay Tories from the 80s often reminisce about how Thatcher's outer office was like Heaven. They loved the flummery and the woman they sometimes called Mother. In the play *Tory Boyz*, James Graham, the playwright/screenwriter, has a Tory aide in a minister's outer office saying "Lesson one, Robert, the Tory Party is the gayest party, by about a country mile. Certainly, behind the scenes, our lot and certainly in London. The whole machine survives on them." But Craig never goes to "leftie political theatre" if he can help it. He's more Shaftesbury Avenue than Islington. However, he knows the back story, though he thinks that generation of careful gays were far too keen to be accepted. Craig is one tough mutha and he wants to be feared. Work on the tabloids has toughened him up. He's got the 'no quarter given and none expected' ethos, the vocabulary of political catchphrases – he blames the woke mob and "the Islington mafia" for practically everything and he's with all the American TV rightists, the Bens, with tropes such as "black privilege".

And the tabloids taught him his value. How he could get away with things by slightly camping them up. And sometimes his editor would say "Here's one for you, Craigie-boy", meaning a hatchet job on a leftie gay activist in which he could write something like "As a gay man myself, I find it frankly embarrassing when X says Y". His old employers often used black writers to attack 'black racism' against white people or brown ones to attack prominent Muslims ("As a Muslim myself, I find it frankly embarrassing..."). This tabloid toughness is the measure of Craig's difference from his older, more genteel gay peers.

He's come a long way from the shy, plump, snaggle-toothed suburban Home Counties boy who originally studied Business Management. From his various employers' view, what's not to like about Craig and his contingent? They make the paper or the station look younger and cooler. The female viewers like him and it's amazing what he can get away with just by putting his particular spin on it. And with his iridescent teeth and skin-tight shiny suits he brightens up the set. Who wants blobby right-wing Tories when they could have Craig?

I'LL TELL YOU ANY TRUTH HE WANTS

12 Straight-Talking Roger

Roger always speaks his mind. We know this because all the separate sub-brands of his multimedia, multi-country deal, press and TV (he's basically an old-media writer/presenter) always say so. There's always some sort of trailer or subtitle to any programme or article of Roger's saying, in so many words, that this particular middle-class man-of-the-people says what he thinks, with no intervening obligation, inhibition or search for political correctness. Or, so it appears, thought. However, like Glenda Slagg, Private Eye's fictional tabloid harridan, who contradicts herself in a few short paras, Roger doesn't always remember what he said a fortnight ago. And doesn't care to be reminded.

When uppity young people challenge him – Roger is in that coming-up-60 area –his increasingly blubbery face distorts into curious configurations and he shouts at the producer afterwards. Which is difficult because the producer, a working Joe on £80,000 a year, knows perfectly well that Roger knows the Big Men/The Power and could get him sacked. Roger always speaks his mind but whose mind exactly is it? He claims, sometimes explicitly, that he is the Voice of the People and that all decent sentient people feel like him about, say, Joe Biden, Meghan Markle, Greta Thunberg or activist trans people. He says they're sometimes too browbeaten by the PC browbeaters, who are literally everywhere, to say so.

If you ask Roger about his politics he says they're all over the place – he's voted this way and that, and admired politicians from different parties. Actually, he sees all politics as showbusiness, so he admires performative politicians and rates them on their ratings. He's the friend of the stars. The fact is that he's been a sort of provincial saloon-bar middle-class Conservative all his life (and as the Conservative Party and his employers have moved sharply rightwards, so has he – it's good for business). He's like his parents in this. They scrabbled enterprisingly to get him into Dotheboys Hall. But not into university. Roger has never been in the 'big ideas' policy wonk business, which he dismisses as pretentious and hypocritical. He's always been out there – in popular media, read and watched by ordinary people. But not, of course, owned by them. When it comes to deal-making, Roger learned early on to go to the top. And his deals have escalated, ever bigger, better and more international. Happily Roger and the various Big Men in his working life have always found themselves in unspoken agreement. Who needs potentially embarrassing policy agreements when both parties know absolutely what the other thinks about Jeremy Corbyn?

Like, say, Boris Johnson – who Roger very much admired, but has been told by the Authorities to tone it down recently – Roger has done a lot of rogering. Despite constant accusations of misogyny and very sloppy thinking, attractive, clever, independent women positively throw themselves at him. Is it the challenge, the fame, the tens of millions a year? ("So what first, Debbie, attracted you to the millionaire Paul Daniels?" the late Caroline Aherne asked Debbie McGee.) Roger, otherwise unmodern, has learned the key 21st-century mechanism: the economic model of being a certain kind of personal media brand is that you must provide constant clickbait and it really doesn't matter when you say 'outrageous' and much complained-of things. Your unspoken agreement absolutely demands you say them; they build the audience. And old notions of shame and disgrace are for the birds. Roger knows The Power has his back. And in any case, Roger, though no intellectual, has completely understood the postmodern idea of making his performances – now you see it, now you don't – part of the show. And leaving people wondering whether he really meant it when he said that unruly women should be incarcerated by popular demand – or was he joking? How exactly should people 'place' him? His accent, clothing choices, large trad houses and other tastes come across as Tim-Nice-But-Dim, boy-done-good or vaguely Sloaney. But he doesn't think of it like that. He feels he's living in the love of the Common People. He knows that, in the unlikely event of him walking along Oxford Street with practically anyone you can name, *they'd recognise him* first. "Roger, you old devil," is what they'd say.

13 Kevin the Lobbyist

Kevin is from Essex. Until he was 18, this seemed a perfectly ordinary state of affairs, as natural as breathing. But at university, and thereafter, he was constantly meeting people who thought it was innately hilarious! In the 1980s (EastEnders!) and 90s, the whole thing about Essex got going – the thing that led to TOWIE in 2010.

At university in London, Kevin realised that lucky young people didn't all go to Oxbridge. He was surrounded by rich kids from absolutely everywhere, but the English ones thought his background – council estate and market trading – was all, in some strange way, cool. Like footballers, casuals and all that. And actually, Kev was cool; he did know about music and he did dress stylishly.

But, above all, he followed America in everything. Like Tom Wolfe's Mid-Atlantic Man, he saw American everything as a way out of the British class trap. He admired the shameless American way of achieving power and money, and later, the American way of doing politics.

By 2003, in his first job in a 'comms agency' (PR and lobbying done the old way), he was the obsessive one who knew all the new tricks from Washington's famous K Street. He'd been there, spending his savings, interning with people who'd never heard of Canvey Island.

One of the first things he learned, before the internet took over politics, was astroturfing, the art of inventing 'grassroots' organisations that spoke up for your clients' concerns seven days a week. Astroturf organisations called things such as 'Americans for this' or 'Mothers for that' popped up on TV and in newspapers in the most useful way, and their spokespeople were media trained to the hilt.

Why didn't we have more of that in Britain? thought Kevin. And why couldn't we get more money into politics? Rich Americans were stuffing anyone and anything that looked useful with real money, literally millions. It made the old British lobbying scandals like 'cash for questions', where MPs got envelopes full of cash, look so puny and pony.

Kevin could see what you could do and he knew that he'd have what's called 'first-mover advantage' if he brought the whole roadshow of media analysts and think tanks (with their impressive quasi-academic line-up of 'fellows') to the UK. K Street lobbyists called think tanks 'wonk whores' because they'd produce impressive-sounding third-party endorsements for their clients' imperatives (less regulation for food manufacturers, lower corporate taxes to encourage industrial investment, etc).

All this American stuff was just brilliant and Britain was wide open, Kevin thought. As he progressed, he became the go-to man in the agency for everything on the internet because he'd seen the potential first. Kevin learned it all assiduously. He'd read economics after all.

He was meeting people, he made himself useful to players in the new government in 2010. And he set up The Agency with Hugo that year.

Hugo was an old Etonian and absolutely brimming with confidence and social capital. He knew David Cameron and Alexander Nix. It was a momentary lapse in self-esteem for Kevin but Hugo was useful and so happy to be bought out for just £10 million in 2018 when the Big Investor came along.

The Big Investor keeps in the background but he knows Kevin can really deliver – he can sell almost any political outcome with his scientific advertising and his ubiquitous spokespeople.

Kevin's got the lot now, including a cream Cubitt villa in prime

Belgravia. And out of London, where people are expecting a McMansion in Loughton of course, he's got a lovely small Lutyens gem in Sussex with a garden designed by Gertrude Jekyll.

When Kevin's not reading the wit and wisdom of Steve Bannon, he's collecting 19th-century first editions with delicious Arts and Crafts bindings.

14 Professor Robert

Prof Robert only rediscovered the residual English working classes, aka the red wallers or the left-behinds or the somewhere people, over the past decade. Until about, say, 2012, he wasn't all that interested in them. They were a bit small beer for his more sweeping global analyses of capitalism. He was more of an ordinary modern history academic then, with successive tenures and attachments, working with colleagues, obeying the rules of statistical reliability and doing thoroughly peer-reviewed things. And earning about £70,000 a year tops.

While fine by most people's lights – putting him in the top 5% of earners – this didn't exactly propel him from his original Home Counties world into the real metropolitan liberal elite, a group he found himself increasingly fascinated by in the Noughties. In those urgent years, he started to look at Britain again and discovered how the real people of this country had been cruelly oppressed by those awful overeducated, overconfident liberal elites and that they were fed up with it.

This elite constantly sneered at modest provincial people. They positively derided people with small-town connections and 'small c' conservative views. Amazingly, as Robert started to put his observations into more mainstream places, he got taken up by those liberal elite types.

First there were the thoughtful centre-left liberals who, surprisingly, were interested in these poor left-behinds and the charge that they were failing them. They asked him to new conferences and onto small-audience TV discussions. They were, so he discovered, completely taken aback by his views. The thought that these tremendously real people drove Brexit was hard to process; the idea of the Bad Elite being turbo-capitalists was fair enough, but to hear that the oppressors were people like them in academia, NGOs and the media was seriously upsetting. Their usual response was that these innocents had been deceived by the right using disinformation and emotive triggers but it was robustly countered by clever Robert.

He said that the liberal elite were contemptuous – the very last thing they wanted to be – of ordinary people's legitimate concerns because they didn't know anything about them! In other words they were saying "Are you calling me stupid?" and "Are you calling me a racist?".

All this slightly uncomfortable early exposure with these junior league liberal elite types, however, led swiftly to something quite different. Robert received a raft of lovely invitations to lovely places in London just as 'Get Brexit done' was being fought out. He'd been talent-spotted by people who ran 'foundations' and 'institutes' who – unlike second-tier universities – seemed to have all the money in the world from absolutely everywhere.

They took him to amazingly smart and expensive London clubs and restaurants. They all said he was absolutely brilliant and tremendously brave to stand out against the dominant academic left-wing orthodoxies, so they wanted to help him spread his findings. They knew people – they always knew lots of people – who'd want him on the boards and councils of well-funded organisations. Things progressed at astonishing speed.

Robert found himself on platforms in Westminster, rather than Salford or Hull. Then he found himself meeting big people from national newspapers. And being introduced to a new media circuitry, joining a discussion with the clever boys from Trigonometry one day and the New Culture Forum, one of his new Tufton Street friends, the next.

And when he went full on into his first big book and tour, those kind newspaper billionaires opened their pages to reveal that the contemptuous cancel culture of university types etc – those metro-politan liberal elites – was ruining the nation.

15 Roddy the 'Economist'

Is Roddy 'an economist'? Not exactly, but then economics is more inexact than anyone ever lets on. The clue's in its rocket science language. But he did get a good degree in economics at an OK second-tier university. He's mostly a journalist – with sabbaticals as a 'fellow' at opaquely funded think tanks here and stints in American universities no one has heard of there. He's had most of the jobs in the manly high-status group of titles newspapers offer. He's been economics editor and business editor at various broadsheets and one tabloid. And deputy political editor earlier. As a child of Thatcher (practically a grandchild because he's still only just in his 50s), he knows how to talk about economics and business in a slightly folksy kitchen cabinet way on TV and radio.

Like Thatcher, he knows how to defend austerity by saying you can't spend what you don't have and how we've piled up a huge post-Covid national debt which will have to be repaid. Someday. Which means we have to look at how we finance public services such as health and involve private capital and commercial operations.

Brexit was wonderful for Roddy because all of media-land was desperate to find plausible economics types who were for it, because most big-league economists absolutely weren't. But, like the leading lights of Economists for Free Trade (Roddy called the leading Brexiteer economist Patrick Minford "heroic"), Roddy was totally up for it. But unlike many of them, Roddy looked nice, wasn't old, starry eyed or noticeably posh, and was reliably entertaining

231

in radio and TV argy-bargys. Just outrageous enough in suggesting that his opponents were ivory-tower theorists who didn't know they were born, without actually mentioning tofu and north London town houses. Or woke. He, by contrast, was deeply ordinaire and even that little bit bloketastic.

Roddy absolutely loved Liz Truss. Or more precisely, he thought she was the right vehicle for the Hayek-on-steroids convictions bubbling beneath his curated commonsensical exterior. He so loved the Truss/Kwarteng budget that he broke the cover of a lifetime and said it was wonderful. This was the moment, he felt, that the Tories got their mojo back. When the Budget went terribly wrong, Roddy blamed liberal commentators. All of Truss's supporters in newspapers, in danger of losing their reputation for doing the most basic sums, lay low. Their editors and broadcasting patrons, meanwhile, were thinking perhaps the man for the job should, in the immediate future, sound just a little more stabilising and constructive, like that nice Jeremy Hunt or that clever Rishi – about both of whom Roddy had written some notably disobliging pieces.

How will he ever get back to being Ace Bloke Economist after they've seen him practically gabbling on TV about the Truss mini-budget being "the first day of the rest of our economic lives"? And later going on to shout that we'd been betrayed by the anti-growth coalition that ran this country behind the scenes – the blobby Treasury mandarins, the academic economists, the progressive eunuchs? How do you row back from there? He found great comfort at the National Conservatism Conference in London, inspired and arranged by some brilliant Americans who plan to do them all across the Western world. He can be loud and proud there.

16 Woke Patrol Willy

Do you know what the woke mob are calling for now? Many among us, distracted by children/household budgets or the imminent prospect of World War Three – and not being at the centre of the policy wonk circuit – might reasonably say 'no'. That's where Willie X, or Woke Patrol Willy, comes in.

It's his job to make sure that op-eds about wokery constantly get written in national newspapers and that high-profile speakers at events such as NatCon UK have terrifying things to report from the woke front.

Willy occupies the metaphorical woke desk at a mid-market tabloid that used to be personed by the 'rogue deb' unit back in the 70s and 80s. Reading that toffs' daughters and major rock stars' sons supported these woke causes, you might reasonably suppose that these were the pet beliefs of people who weren't remotely like you, the reader. They were people so lucky they didn't know they were born.

Woke Patrol Willy had always been drawn to extremists and their battiest manifestoes and sayings. Back in the day as a-self-conscious boy right-winger/ poseur at Durham (but looking and sounding like an Oxbridge wag) back in the late 80s he would penetrate the hard left to get the goods – they let him in because they often believed his views were 'ironic' or 'postmodern' (because nobody could say those things seriously, could they?).

Later he specialised in 'loonie-left' pieces across the national newspapers, revealing the maddest-sounding views of the craziest East London councillors. But when the new woke tropes and memes started appearing in American media, Willy changed his tune. This woke stuff seemed to him to out-mad anything, say, Jeremy Corbyn had ever said, and to have the great additional advantage of dividing the left. Older leftists found the woke priorities and vocabulary – particularly the trans stuff – mystifying and maddening (can we please get back to a proper class war?).

When Willy's column 'Woke Patrol' got going, he got an inbox full of stories from the kinds of people who'd sent him loonie-leftist stories 20 years before. Many were by then oldies shopping their children and grandchildren to the authorities. Others were older academics – conventionally right and left leaning – who feared that their little charges might cancel them any minute.

Soon 'Woke Patrol' became one of the most-read columns in the paper, widely quoted. Willy was constantly on the TV with his stories. His slightly theatrical delivery gave his appearances extra welly. His long pauses, rolling eyes and fastidious pronunciation of ridiculous-sounding organisations' names were almost as reliable as, say, a funny story from Gyles Brandreth.

The woke stories were about race, gender, colonialism, statue-defacing and the allegedly crazed indoctrinations doled out by woke schoolteachers and academics. The paper sometimes gave money for particularly lurid stories about teachers who said unpatriotic things.

The gender thing proved particularly popular. According to Willy's correspondents, children – tiny tots actually – were being taught that there were lots of genders to choose from. Willy was keen on asking politicians, for instance, to define what a woman was and wasn't. Many of these questions inevitably came down to the legitimate possession of a penis, and whether people with one could be allowed into 'women's spaces'. Willy devoted many column inches to this subject, provoking gales of uneasy laughter.

His grown-up children wished he'd give it a rest but, like many journalists working this particular beat, he knew it was what the public wanted – and what his employers loved and rewarded.

Which was why his fellow wags on the paper now call Willie X Willy with a 'y'.

Tory Tovarich
WEALTH
MANAGEMENT
ARREST
ROOM

PROSPECTUS проспект

17 Alex: A Friend to the Russians

Alex is a worried man: he worries about being named and shamed, he worries about his ultra-sensitive files being hacked, and he worries about experiencing a variety of possible life-shortening incidents (defenestration, poisoning, being run over in Gloucester Road).

A few years ago, he was at the top of a very profitable tree. He was one of those suave, handsome, coming-up-50 professionals who've helped Russians and other global super-rich types with their important business in London – their companies, houses, lawsuits, and their lobbying. They helped transfer Russian money to all kinds of commercially and politically useful people in Westminster – individual politicians and their parties, journalists, influencers, think tanks and more besides.

What could've been a smarter job than his in, say, 2011, before the Skripal poisoning, the Ukrainian invasion and the stories about Boris Johnson and Evgeny Lebedev? When Tory politicians were proud to belong to Conservative Friends of Russia (it's been dismantled now)? When connected PR firms and lawyers were coining it and some big players seemed to be evolving into a new hybrid called 'reputation management'? Lawyers who started from the idea of through-the-line personal and corporate brand projection and protection – rather than just wigs-for-hire?

Rich Russians were everywhere. Buying overpriced tennis games with prime ministers. Hosting extravagant parties at a level which dwarfed the home-grown kind. Getting their little darlings into public schools (where, according to schoolmasters, they sometimes continued their various parents' vendettas in very violent ways). And suing the arse off anyone who criticised them through their clever London lawyers (it's called SLAPPs).

Most of all, they were urging us on to Brexit. Who should be in Johnson and Marina's kitchen – with Michael Gove and Sarah Vine back in early 2016 when Boris was wrestling with whether or not to come out for Brexit – but Evgeny Lebedev, son of KGB-trained Alexander? It was delicious for Alex as a corporate PR/lobbyist with a legal background, altogether fantastic contacts and a 'refreshing' lack of those old-school inhibitions about his new clients. It validated him. "So 20th century, so Little Englander," he used to say. Alex employed Russians, even started learning Russian, and opened a small gateway office in Moscow. He was completely on the list.

The Deripaska yacht incident of August 2008 involving George Osborne, Peter Mandelson, banker Nat Rothschild and Oleg Deripaska – then said to be Russia's richest man – served to show just what exotic power-broker configurations the new London–Moscow global endeavour could pull together. Slow people wondered who was doing what to whom in that story, but Alex just thought proudly "this is my world".

While Alex saw himself as part of the white heat generated by the new masters of the universe, there's no doubt that his new clients saw him as an English gent straight out of the films – somewhere between Hugh Grant, Benedict Cumberbatch and Colin Firth.

He had connections, some his own, others through his wife (the granddaughter of an earl). He knew people with absurdly beautiful houses around the country (many had been used as locations for films). His toff connections in those houses adored the Russians, with their marvellous money and their amusing directness ("How much is this house?"). So what wasn't to like?

Gradually, however – after Skripal, after those crucial books and investigations: Catherine Belton and Oliver Bullough, Carole

Cadwalladr and Tom Burgis – Alex started to detect what a spokesperson for Evgeny Lebedev recently called "the hallmarks of anti-Russian racist harassment". They emerged among ordinary centre-right people he met; he sensed the change. He knew they'd seen *McMafia*.

Then there were the incidents in which various significant Russians in English exile had died in strange circumstances. The most unlikely people had apparently hanged themselves. A shocked friend had described to him finding a dead man impaled on railings in a smart London square. The man had turned out to be a British entrepreneur/fixer who the papers said had some allegedly dodgy dealings in Moscow with some particularly difficult people. His family had claimed that he'd been killed. That was a bit closer to home.

But now, Oliver Bullough's brilliant *Butler to the World* (describing London's smart Russia helpers – among others) and the recent Channel 4 *Dispatches* into Boris and the Lebedevs has made Alex and his kind obvious marks for investigative journalists wanting to make their names. He dreads the call. And some of his key clients were sanctioned in 2022, which meant cash flow problems.

He remembers, somewhat bitterly, a dinner party seven years ago – fantastic food and wine in a billionaire house on Cheyne Walk – with fellow collaborators (more lawyers and financial types who worked for Eastern Europeans). They'd joked about the next big idea/service they could offer their clients: a witness protection service for the super-rich...

18 The Boys in the Special Ops Room

Back in the old world, after months of misery looking at Labour's persistent poll lead, and seeing nothing but the prospect of it lengthening, the boys – they're mainly boys – in the Special Operations Room have just seen a blinding light.

Those boys are a fascinating group. Young and youngish, from a variety of backgrounds, from semi-toff to downright Australian! They're very focused and many of them wear serious specs. Some of them need to Get a Life, but they so love their work. And some of them have a soft spot for Jordan Peterson.

But what they all have in common is an absolute belief in American 'political technology' as taught in the great lobbying academies of K Street, Washington. They love the sheer profession-alism of this kind of politics.

Their lodestars are the hugely – but opaquely – funded US Conservative think tanks: this institute and that foundation. But the people who fund them know what they're going to say – because they've paid for it. This strong Anglo-American right-wing linkage is central to the Special Operations Room. It is a group devoted to keeping the Conservatives in power forever. (Dominic Cummings, ahead of his time, was blogging about how Tories needed those clever US ideas back in 2004. But the boys feel very disappointed by his recent behaviour.)

They've encouraged – at a distance – Nigel Farage's and Suella Braverman's campaign of small boat watching, knowing that words like 'invasion' go down nicely. Immigration of all kinds is a constant in the culture wars. And they subtly endorsed the platforming of women – particularly leftist ones – who seem to be fighting the trans ideology wing of the woke mob with the help of the mostly Tory national press. 'Trans' is all tied in with cancel culture – meaning that terrible woke mob that is constantly accused by useful organisations like Toby Young's Free Speech Union of shutting up/banning/de-platforming brave souls like actor Laurence Fox.

There was always some hope there, because some identity politics activists – minority people with no real power at all – often said the most *ridiculous* things. The sorts of things reporters on the woke mob desks on national newspapers loved to report, to make their readers shiver in their shoes in Bournemouth. *These people could be coming after you!*

But the Tories persisted in shooting themselves in the foot every time. And over more important issues practically everyone seemed to care about (mortgages, the cost of living). And then – oh joy unconfined, custard with everything. The Special Operations Room recognised what'd been staring them in the face forever: they needed to take it to the environmentalists and kill several fat birds with one stone. Environmentalists – the people behind net zero and related campaigns – are obviously making the world even harder for hard-pressed ordinary folk (like the owners of polluting old bangers potentially banned from travelling) – folk who aren't absolutely convinced about global warming.

Researchers sifting through Keir Starmer's dustbins in the unlikely hope of finding something really exciting were redeployed to finding out the cost of scrapping your gas boiler in favour of hugely expensive heat pumps.

Environmentalists – how could they have missed this? – are so obviously *not like us*. They're so abstract, so outrageously middle class, internationalist and overeducated. They don't know they're born, as Lee Anderson might say. They might talk a good line and blind us with 'science' but when did George Monbiot last have to weigh up a BOGOF at Asda? Was Caroline Lucas ever a dinner lady?

Exciting possibilities immediately presented themselves for the great American lobbyists' art of astroturfing through organisations led by a Maxine Peake type in the northern chapter and someone more Ilford sounding for the south. The full horror of crazed environmentalists could just be today's equivalent of flinging a 'dead cat' on the table – the favourite conversation-stopper of Sir Lynton Crosby, the Australian political campaigner absolutely worshipped by the boys in the Special Operations Room. He's the one who did Johnson's campaigns for London Mayor. But it's a dangerous game.

If global warming is as imminently world boiling as those obviously foreign clever dicks in the UN say it is, it could catch out politicians who do more than ignore it but actively lie about it. They could get it in the neck pretty soon.

Afterword

I've had a long-standing disagreement with a friend. It's about the trans issue. She's a feminist, but not by profession – nor an academic either. She's a widow with three children and a London 'tastemaker' who runs a profitable little business, so she's spent her life around visually smart people, in smart London places, with lots of gay men and women. But when the trans issue comes up, all bets are off. She's convinced that there's a plot against women – as in absolutely 'cis' ones – and it's a plot to destroy all the things they've achieved in her lifetime, including sport. (She's so *not* a sportswoman!) And along with the sports thing goes, according to my friend, a cancel culture shutdown on any criticism of the trans-activist mob she believes exists.

I ask her where she got this curious phrase, and she looks irritated, as if I'm about to launch into some fraudulent 'logic'.

"So who are these people anyway?" I ask her. "And how many of them are there?

"That so isn't the point," she says.

Ever the swot, I've looked up the trans figures from the last census. And, as you might expect, the numbers are *tiny* even after all the problems with the Tavistock Institute's Gender Identity Unit allegedly pushing confused young people into transitioning – so it looks like something that doesn't begin to warrant all this drama.

But somebody *has* made a drama of it. Lee Anderson's famous admission that Conservatives would have to fight the 2024 election in part on trans issues lets *that* cat out of the bag.

At the core of many of the culture wars stories is something said or done by somebody who has no idea of how media really works and no idea how a skilled culture wars team can run away with them and their ideas. An obscure academic with no power, money or access to big media, or an activist in a small pressure group formerly on the margins who gets picked up by the quote machine. They're likely to have said something seriously silly that sounds – especially with expert editing – truly mad, deeply annoying and very memorable. But if its importance seems endorsed by at least part of the mainstream media and if, even now, most of us assume that it wouldn't be on, say, *Good Morning Britain* if there was absolutely nothing to it (like the idea that there are activists, including school-teachers, absolutely everywhere, insisting there are 100 genders) it gets under the skin, and it's out there. All the culture warriors need to do is exaggerate it a thousandfold and get us talking about it.

So, going back to those big questions I was taught in my first job, a) who exactly is doing/saying this extraordinary thing? and, b) how many of them are there? And there's the other vital question, c) *who's paying for this?* – because storytelling at scale, and sustained over months and years, costs big money (ask major advertisers!) And who benefits? It could be a financial or a political benefit for an individual or an organisation, like a political party. Or for people who are very un-keen on fossil-fuel cutbacks.

When you read or hear something startling in the culture wars arena – not the rational/checkable price-of-fish sort of question – you need to start by asking who's talking, who exactly is bringing you this story and, of course, where they belong politically, culturally and financially (always follow the connections!). Who actually owns the platform you've read or heard it on? What's the track record of the think tank involved? What do the various 'trans-parency' scrutineers like Transparify and DeSmog say about them? Where are they coming from? What are their connections? You can work out, for instance, where Russell Brand is at now on many issues by the extreme company he keeps on screen.

Once you've done that sort of deep dive on one story – I know you're thinking "get a life" but if it concerns you, confuses you, upsets you, starts you shouting it's worth pursuing – you'll start to recognise culture warriors for who and what they are, and how their interests/their clients' interests align. And you'll realise *they all seem to know each other. Every one of the stories at the core of this book is connected to the rest.* The same scary writers, the same newspapers and sites, the same lobbyists and think tanks, the same rich American allies, the same political friends in high places. Who's on whose advisory board? Who's on whose panel discussion platform? Who's being interviewed on whose YouTube channels? You need to get your eye in, and then you can persuade your friends and family.

The fact remains, however, that these sorts of issues are the ones that divide friends and families – and whole countries – precisely because they're so expertly communicated and they go in far below our rational defences into our emotional core. There's nothing more infuriating for women than mansplaining which ignores the real issues. You can't just disabuse people with rational argument and fact-checking, and you can't shout them out of it. What you can do is understand where they're coming from and why they believe that Muslims want to take over the country, or eco-zealots want to impose all sorts of restrictions *just for the sake of it*. Or why they think protestors are actually all privileged elite types. And then you can show them how to assess something they care about for themselves so they can get in the habit.

It's all difficult stuff and the results are often disappointing. Impatient people say you should be taking the fight to the warriors and fighting fire with fire (and not being shy of putting pressure on social media companies). But the soggy centre/centre left are disadvantaged against the professionals because they lack the shameless focus and casual relationship with the truth you need for this kind of storytelling. And they don't know how to raise money and recruit skills for their stories. And they won't easily get taken up by media unless they change their tune (or, for the BBC, tone it right down, don't name names – and for other mainstream broadcasters 'keep it simple'; audiences can only take so much reality).

It was hard for the opposition back then and, as Andrew Neil pointed out in a curious piece in the *Daily Mail* earlier in 2024,[243] although the ultra-cautious Labour Party already looked likely to win this year's UK general election (and did, driving the Conservatives to their worst seat count in history) – and he was so right: the rest of the world, starting with Europe and the USA, was clearly pointing in the opposite direction. They still seem to be going towards eventually having far-right/populist governments with strongman leaders. The implication clearly was that Labour's triumph would be short lived. The UK right would regroup to form something that – whatever it was called – would more closely resemble France's National Rally or Hungary's Fidesz. A more clearly populist party, animated by the ideas of enemies within (the woke mob) and outside – the 'invaders' storming our beaches – and the idea of the liberal elite, the ones who've taken over everything, was serving as a common factor in the *Daily Hate*. Especially if those elites were in London.

Brits think of themselves as uniquely pragmatic, uniquely resistant to lurid ideas. The idea of 'common sense' was once central to our public life. But for three years we lived with a narcissistic fantasist as our prime minister and ignored the early warnings because he was amusing. Boris Johnson greatly admires Donald Trump – it's mutual: Trump called him "Trump Britain" – and Johnson, in turn, endorses him for the next US election.[244] People who are paid to study these things say the US is nearer to a civil war after the November '24 election – whatever the outcome – than it's been since the last one (1861–5). And that's because a huge and enraged minority of American voters – larger than in 2021 – believe the lie constantly retold that the 2020 election was stolen by the Democrats. As James Davison Hunter, the original *Culture Wars* author, said recently, another US civil war still isn't a certainty... but you never get one without a culture war first.[245]

Acknowledgements

I've talked to a variety of clever people with inside knowledge about how culture wars are done. Some were understandably un-keen to be named, because they want to retain access to touchy top people – or just keep their jobs! Others told me about the context and changes in culture war thinking from the 20th century to the 21st.

I want to thank Martin Rowson for dramatising the main points of the stories and characters with his brilliant drawings, often before I'd really grasped them myself (see little Liz Truss outside the IEA!). It helps that he's been around so many of those blocks himself, and he's met many of the protagonists.

My home team of Maxine Ostwald, Liz Hills and Georgina Jackson managed me throughout, and made everything look and sound better and more accurate. They researched and footnoted a huge range of these subjects, from Piers Morgan to carbon capture. The indefatigable Liz Gerard (@gameoldgirl on X/Twitter) provided the tabloid headlines that follow each 'story' chapter.

My agent Adrian Sington of Kruger Cowne for providing unfailingly good advice!

I've talked to a fair few profs, people who know their subjects over time and across the world – the opposite of the journalistic approach. I've tried out my more speculative ideas on them and generated useful context for the ones that survived. Professor Patrick Barwise, co-author of our recent *War Against the BBC* and co-discoverer of the fascinating 'Defund the BBC' initiative, started me on the prof hunt.

Professor Steven Barnett and Dr Douglas Specht of the University of Westminster conducted the analysis of Defund the BBC's online launch which I draw on in Chapter 4.

Professor Brian Cathcart of Kingston University and Professor Julian Petley of Brunel University helped me understand the background of some great media issues. The Media Reform Coalition, and particularly Professor Tom Mills of Aston University, have analysed the extraordinary patterns of UK media ownership and affiliations to set out the context for absolutely everything in our curious media ecology.

Robert Ford, Professor of Political Science at the University of Manchester, Sam Friedman, Professor of Sociology at the London School of Economics, and Danny Dorling, Professor of Geography at University of Oxford all helped me understand the issues in defining 'elites', a favourite preoccupation of culture warriors.

Sociologists Dr Sheena MacRae of Anglia Ruskin University and Dr Huw Davies of the University of Edinburgh have written a brilliant and forensic analysis for the Institute of Race Relations: 'An Anatomy of the British War on Woke', which nails culture warriors' initiatives and linkages; I have drawn on their ideas constantly. George Monbiot is eternally vigilant on the trajectory of influencers like Russell Brand and the Claire Fox tendency over time, and helped me understand what drives them on.

Michael Crick, Nigel Farage's first 'grown-up' biographer, helped me to nail some crucial detail about that eternally interesting man. Catherine Bennett of the *Guardian* has followed the weaponisation and demonisation of Harry and Meghan and was most helpful. Andy Beckett, also of the *Guardian*, has been following everything that matters forever, and was illuminating about the National Conservatism Conference.

There's a cluster of *Byline Times* contributors who turned out to know a lot that I didn't about the politics of race and faith, including Dr Nafeez Ahmed and Karam Bales. Peter Oborne, who's followed the truth to his own disadvantage over the last decade, studies these questions closely.

Old friends from my 'Indy' days, particularly Yasmin Alibhai-

Brown and Sally-Ann Lasson, talked things through (and, bravely, read things through). Playwright Tim Fountain reminded me of his hilarious play about Toby Young.

Peter Geoghegan, former editor in chief of OpenDemocracy, wrote Britain's answer to Jane Mayer's seminal *Dark Money*. His *Democracy for Sale* is a key reminder of how Americanised our politics has become. Matt d'Ancona of the *New European* wrote the crucial essay on the reality of 21st-century Conservatism, 'Bannon's Britain', which I re-read constantly.

Nick North, the BBC's audience research guru, filled in some important gaps about audience behaviour. Claire Enders, doyenne of media analysts, helped me understand the UK's new broadcasters. Leo Hickman of Carbon Brief told me about gases and particles.

Finally, there's the team at Byline, thrusting into national newsagents and grocery chains and going global. Founders Peter Jukes and Stephen Colegrave, Hardeep Matharu, editor of *Byline Times*, where my 'Metropolitan Illiberal Elite' and 'Doors' pieces were originally published, Ella Baddeley, Matthew Gallagher and my *very* global editor Kyle Taylor all asked the right questions.

Endnotes

1 The group consisted of Carl Grunberg, Georg Lukacs, Karl Korsch, Karl August Wittfogel and Friedrich Pollock. See the Marxists Internet Archive, https://www.marxists.org/subject/frankfurt-school/index.htm

2 List of media workers ineligible for employment because of alleged communist or subversive ties, generated by Hollywood Studios in the late 1940s and 50s: https://www.britannica.com/topic/Hollywood-blacklist

3 Marie Brenner, 'How Donald Trump and Roy Cohn's Ruthless Symbiosis Changed America', *Vanity Fair*, 28 June 2017.

4 Director Marianne Elliott. "I couldn't sleep, I'm busy dying." Roy Cohn portrayed by Nathan Lane, *Angels in America*, National Theatre, 2018, https://www.youtube.com/watch?v=eLhq8jt4p3Q&ab_channel=NationalTheatre

5 Patrick Joseph Buchanan, 'Culture War Speech: Address to the Republican National Convention', *Voices of Democracy* 39, 17 August 1992.

6 *Things Fell Apart*, BBC Radio 4 series by Jon Ronson.

7 Jane Mayer, *Dark Money*, Chapter 2, 'The Hidden Hand: Richard Mellon Scaife', Scribe Publications, 2016, p. 80.

8 Adam Bychawski, 'Revealed: Truss-allied think tank met dozens of MPs prior to leadership win', *Open Democracy*, 11 January 2023, https://www.opendemocracy.net/en/institute-of-economic-affairs-liz-truss-2022-accounts/

9 Matthew d'Ancona, 'Bannon's Britain', Tortoise Media, 28 September 2019, https://www.tortoisemedia.com/2019/09/28/bannons-britain/

10 Carole Cadwalladr, Boris Johnson, Steve Bannon texts foreign secretary resignation speech', *Guardian*, 22 June 2019, https://www.theguardian.com/politics/2019/jun/22/boris-johnson-steve-bannon-texts-foreign-secretary-resignation-speech

11 Steve Bannon in Rome on 25 March 2019. In an earlier interview with the journalist Michael Lewis, Bannon said, "The Democrats don't matter, The real opposition is the media. And the way to deal with them is to flood the zone with shit."

12 Francesca Gillett, 'Conservatives need a bigger bazooka, Truss tells US right-wing event', BBC News, 23 February 2024, https://www.bbc.co.uk/news/uk-politics-68376802

13 Holly Patrick, 'Liz Truss did "nothing wrong" over Tommy Robinson "hero" comment, Tory minister says', *Independent*, 28 February 2024, https://www.

independent.co.uk/tv/news/liz-truss-tommy-robinson-deep-state-b2503798.html

14 YouGov, 'Share Your Opinion on Liz Truss', disliked by 66%, March 2024, https://yougov.co.uk/topics/politics/explore/public_figure/Liz_Truss

15 Matthew d'Ancona, op. cit.

16 Intelligence and Security Committee of Parliament; 'Russia' – Russian Expatriates, pp. 15, 49.

17 George Monbiot, 'How US billionaires are fuelling the hard-right cause in Britain', *Guardian*, 7 December 2018, https://www.theguardian.com/commentisfree/2018/dec/07/us-billionaires-hard-right-britain-spiked-magazine-charles-david-koch-foundation

18 Media Reform Coalition, *Ownership Report 2023, Who Owns the UK Media?*, https://www.mediareform.org.uk/wp-content/uploads/2023/10/MRC-Who-Owns-The-UK-Media-2023-V3.3.pdf

19 Suzanne Goldenberg, 'Greenpeace exposes sceptics hired to cast doubt on climate science', *Guardian*, 8 December 2015, https://www.theguardian.com/environment/2015/dec/08/greenpeace-exposes-sceptics-cast-doubt-climate-science

20 Jamie Grierson, 'Labour questions Dominic Cummings's links to Russia', *Guardian*, 3 November 2019, https://www.theguardian.com/politics/2019/nov/03/dominic-cummings-labour-questions-russia-links

21 Rowena Mason, 'Dominic Cummings think-tank called for end of BBC in current form', *Guardian*, 21 January 2020, https://www.theguardian.com/politics/2020/jan/21/dominic-cummings-thinktank-called-for-end-of-bbc-in-current-form

22 The Wayback Machine is a popular internet archive where users can explore more than 866 billion web pages that have been saved over time: https://archive.org/web/

23 Jack Holmes, 'Behold the Tucker Carlson Interview Where He Got Owned So Bad He Refused to Air It', *Esquire*, 20 February 2019, https://www.esquire.com/news-politics/a26432056/tucker-carlson-fox-news-interview-rutger-bergman/

24 Jemima McEvoy, 'Tucker Carlson Made as Much as $20 Million a Year at Fox News', *Forbes*, 24 April 2023, https://www.forbes.com/sites/jemimamcevoy/2023/04/24/tucker-carlson-made-as-much-as-20-million-a-year-at-fox-news/

25 Helene Mulholland, 'Johnson condemned for describing £250,000 deal as "chicken feed", *Guardian*, 14 July 2009.

26 Kathryn S. Olmsted, 'Beaverbrook', Aspects of History, https://aspectsofhistory.com/beaverbrook/

27 *Spitting Image* was a British satirical television puppet show, created by Peter Fluck, Roger Law and Martin Lambie-Naire, first broadcast in 1984.

28 *PressGazette*, 7 November 2023, https://pressgazette.co.uk/publishers/broadcast/gb-news-shareholders-farage-wootton/

29 Jim Waterson, 'Rivals plan Fox News-style opinionated TV station in UK', *Guardian*, 29 August 2020, https://www.theguardian.com/media/2020/aug/29/rivals-plan-fox-news-style-opinionated-tv-station-in-uk

30 Ellie Harrison, 'Jeremy Clarkson Documentary Tells Story Behind Moment He Punched Piers Morgan Three Times', *Independent*, 30 January 2023.

31 Kitty Chrisp, 'A timeline of Jeremy Clarkson's annual A-Level tweets to inspire and enrage you depending on how you look at it', *Metro*, 17 August 2023, https://metro.co.uk/2023/08/17/results-day-a-timeline-of-jeremy-clarksons-a-level-tweets-19347991/

32 Jonathan Sale, 'An Education in the Life of Piers Morgan', *Independent*, 8 May 2008, https://www.independent.co.uk/student/career-planning/getting-job/an-education-in-the-life-of-piers-morgan-822519.html

33 Quoted from George Monbiot, 'It's a tragedy of modern plutocratic Britain: if you want to rise, follow the Piers Morgan playbook', *Guardian*, 15 September 2023. https://www.theguardian.com/commentisfree/2023/sep/15/tragedy-modern-britain-piers-morgan-playbook

34 Quoted from Sky News, 'Jeremy Clarkson's Sun column about Meghan was sexist, press watchdog rules', 30 June 2023.

35 Georgia Aspinall, 'Here's the Story behind Jeremy Clarkson's Strange Obsession with Meghan Markle', *Grazia Daily*, 12 July 2023, https://graziadaily.co.uk/life/in-the-news/what-did-jeremy-clarkson-say-about-meghan-markle-sun-comments/

36 Strategic Lawsuit Against Public Participation.SLAPPs are legal actions typically brought by corporations or individuals with the intention of harassing, intimidating and financially or psychologically exhausting opponents via improper use of the legal system.

37 Judiciary UK: *Banks v. Cadwalladr*. "As the judge held, the claimant proved that the publication of the TED Talk caused serious harm. The claimant thereby satisfied that threshold test and established the wrong in question.", 28 February 2023, p.9 [38(1)].

38 Kim Renfro and Lauren Edmonds, 'A complete timeline of how Piers Morgan met Meghan Markle and went from publicly singing her praises to trashing her on TV', *Business Insider*, 14 December 2022. https://www.businessinsider.com/piers-morgan-meghan-markle-relationship-interview-timeline?r=US&IR=T

39 Piers Morgan, 'Congratulations Harry, you've picked a real keeper', *Daily Mail*, 27 November 2017. https://www.dailymail.co.uk/news/article-5121713/PIERS-MORGAN-Congrats-Harry-pal-Meghan-keeper.html

40 Tom Bowers, *Revenge: Meghan, Harry and the War between the Windsors*, Blink Publishing, 2022.

41 Allister Heath, 'Harry and Meghan's Netflix "Documentary" is an Egregious Betrayal', *Telegraph*, 14 December 2022.

42 Jacey Fortin, 'Critical Race Theory: A Brief History', *New York Times*, 8 November 2021, https://www.nytimes.com/article/what-is-critical-race-theory.html

43 Peter Sheridan and Caroline Graham, 'Perhaps it'd be easier if I was dead, heartbroken Thomas Markle says his daughter is ignoring him and has changed all her numbers since marrying Harry... but he WON'T let the Palace silence him', *Daily Mail*, 28 July 2018.

44 Archie Bland, 'Piers Morgan will find many ways to deny phone hacking – but how long before his number is up?', Guardian, 18 December 2023, https://www.theguardian.com/commentisfree/2023/dec/18/piers-morgan-phone-hacking-mirror-editor-judge-prince-harry
45 Tom Pilgrim, 'Judge accepts evidence that Piers Morgan knew about phone hacking at The Mirror', Independent, 15 December 2023, https://www.independent.co.uk/news/uk/crime/piers-morgan-omid-scobie-justice-kylie-minogue-mirror-group-newspapers-b2464820.html
46 Rachel Johnson, 'Sorry Harry, but your beautiful bolter had failed my Mum Test', Daily Mail, 6 November 2016.
47 Melanie McDonagh, 'Prince Harry and Meghan Markle, the Union of Royalty and Showbiz', Spectator, November 2017, https://www.spectator.co.uk/article/prince-harry-and-meghan-markle-the-union-of-royalty-and-showbiz/ 27
48 Ellie Hall, 'Here Are 20 Headlines Comparing Meghan Markle to Kate Middleton That May Show Why She and Prince Harry Left Royal Life', Buzzfeed News, 13 January 2020, https://www.buzzfeednews.com/article/ellievhall/meghan-markle-kate-middleton-double-standards-royal
49 Tanya Gold, 'Calling Someone a Gammon is Hate Speech', GQ, 16 May 2018, https://www.gq-magazine.co.uk/article/what-does-gammon-mean
50 Migration Watch UK, Channel Crossing Tracker, https://www.migrationwatchuk.org/channel-crossings-tracker
51 Mark Duell and Eirian Jane Prosser, 'Furious locals launch protest in Dorset as Bibby Stockholm barrage that will house 500 male asylum seekers arrives at port in the popular seaside resort', Daily Mail, 18 July 2023, https://www.dailymail.co.uk/news/article-12309721/Furious-locals-launch-protest-Dorset-Bibby-Stockholm-barge-house-500-male-asylum-seekers-gets-set-arrive-port-popular-seaside-resort-today.html
52 Sarah Marsh, 'Steve Bannon calls for Tommy Robinson to be released from prison', Guardian, 15 July 2018, https://www.theguardian.com/us-news/2018/jul/15/steve-bannon-tommy-robinson-released-from-prison-trump-strategist-lbc-radio-interview
53 Pamela Brown, 'Trump pardons Steve Bannon as one of his final acts in office', CNN, 20 January 2021.
54 The English Defence League (EDL) is a far-right Islamophobic organisation in England.
55 Merseyside Police, '15 arrested: update following violent disorder in Knowsley', 11 February 2023, https://www.merseyside.police.uk/news/merseyside/news/2023/february/15-arrested-update-following-violent-disorder-in-knowsley/
56 Matthew d'Ancona, op. cit.
57 Adam Forrest, 'Double blow for Rishi Sunak as party deputy chair quits in Rwanda rebellion', Independent, 16 January 2024, https://www.independent.co.uk/news/uk/politics/lee-anderson-sacked-sunak-rwanda-bill-b2479669.html
58 Migration Watch UK – see note 51.
59 George Parker, Sebastian Payne et al., 'Inside Boris Johnson's Money Network', Financial Times, 30 July 2021, https://www.ft.com/content/8c6041ff-a223-43e9-9e45-53c3f7cf47f7

60 ECHR, *The Council of Europe*, Chapter 8: Presidents of the Commission, p. 3, https://www.echr.coe.int/documents/d/echr/anni_book_chapter08_eng

61 See https://twitter.com/DefundBBC

62 Defund the BBC, TV, press, radio, https://www.defundbbc.uk/tv-press-radio/ – James Yucel speaking on Talk Radio, 8 June 2020.

63 Yasmin IRufo, Ian Youngs & Steven McIntosh, 'Dan Wootton no longer employed by GB News after Ofcom ruling', 5 March 2024, https://www.bbc.co.uk/news/entertainment-arts-68470283

64 James Bickerton, 'New campaign to "Defund the BBC" seesexplosion in support after launch', *Daily Express*, 11 June 2020, https://www.express.co.uk/news/uk/1294308/BBC-News-Campaign-Defund-the-BBC-licence-fee-payments

65 Steven Barnett and Doug Specht, '#DefundtheBBC: the anatomy of a social media campaign', The Conversation, 10 June 2020, https://theconversation.com/defundthebbc-the-anatomy-of-a-social-media-campaign-140391

66 Glasgow University Conservative & Unionist Association announcement, Facebook, 20 July 2020, https://www.facebook.com/GUTories/posts/3145214278896343/

67 This website has now been taken down.

68 James Yucel, 'What will the DUP do next?', *Glasgow Guardian*, 10 December 2019.

69 James Yucel, 'The Draining Life of a Young Conservative', *The Critic*, 15 May 2021, https://thecritic.co.uk/the-draining-life-of-a-young-conservative/

70 Tim Fenton, 'Student BBC basher WORKS FOR THE TORIES', Zelo Street, 9 June 2020, https://zelo-street.blogspot.com/2020/06/student-bbc-basher-works-for-tories.html

71 Rebecca Perring, 'BBC Crisis: "Defund the BBC" campaign raise £30K in boycott bid – not fit for purpose', *Daily Express*, 15 July 2020, https://www.express.co.uk/news/uk/1309908/bbc-news-defund-bbc-tv-licence-row-bbc-latest

72 See https://order-order.com/2020/07/06/defund-the-bbc/

73 Steve Anglesey, 'The Brexiteers behind the "Defund the BBC" campaign', *The New European*, 30 July 2020, https://www.theneweuropean.co.uk/brexit-news-steve-anglesey-defund-the-bbc-campaign-87818/

74 Ciaran McGrath, Liam Doyle and Max Parry, 'Huw Edwards named by his own wife as BBC presenter at centre of sex pictures scandal', *Daily Express*, 12 July 2023, https://www.express.co.uk/news/uk/1789405/BBC-presenter-named-explicit-pictures

75 Jimmy Savile was a regular BBC presenter from 1964 to 1988; however, his last BBC job was co-presenting the music show *Top of the Pops* in 2006.

76 Christopher Hope, 'Rory Stewart bids to become National Trust's chairman as it reels from "woke" agenda claims', *Telegraph*, 15 October 2021.

77 Max Colbet, 'Tufton Street Linked Restore Trust Sees Surge in Funding from Undisclosed Donors', *Byline Times*, 24 January 2024, https://bylinetimes.com/2024/01/24/tufton-street-linked-restore-trust-sees-surge-in-funding-from-undisclosed-donors/

78 Restore Trust, 'The effect of the Quick Vote on democracy in The

National Trust', December 2023, https://static1.squarespace.com/static/60a3e3bb411b976850808785/t/6571b7424f2b5907a714ebce/1701951304087/Restore+Trust+Report+-+The+effect+of+the+Quick+Vote+on+democracy+in+the+National+Trust+2023+vFINAL.pdf

79 Simon Heffer, 'The National Trust has an agenda – skewing history so it's anti-British', *Telegraph*, 14 October 2022, https://www.telegraph.co.uk/news/2022/10/14/zewditu-gebreyohanes-interview-national-trust-has-agenda-skewing/

80 See Market Screener, https://in.marketscreener.com/insider/NEIL-RECORD-A09XQY/.

81 Tom Harris, 'Neil Record: Life Vice President and Former Chair of the IEA Board Trustees', The IEA, 17 March 2023, https://iea.org.uk/helpie_faq/neil-record-life-vice-president-and-former-chair-of-the-iea-board-of-trustees/.

82 Joe Sommerlad, 'What is 55 Tufton Street? The house that crashed the UK economy', *Independent*, 18 October 2022, https://www.independent.co.uk/news/uk/politics/what-is-55-tufton-street-b2205193.html

83 City AM, 19 October 2023, 'UK Entrepreneurs see Labour as "party of business"', https://www.cityam.com/uk-entrepreneurs-prefer-labour-as-party-of-business-survey-finds/

84 Rosamund Urwin, Charlotte Wace and Paul Morgan-Bentley, 'Russell Brand Accused of Rape, Sexual Assaults and Abuse', *Times*, 16 September 2023, https://www.thetimes.co.uk/article/russell-brand-rape-sexual-assault-abuse-allegations-investigation-v5hxdlmb6

85 Lottie Kilraine, 'What is Rumble? The video platform "immune to cancel culture" and used by Russell Brand', ITV News, 22 September 2023.

86 Peter Jukes and Hardeep Matharu, 'Editorial: The Populist Brand', *Byline Times*, 22 September 2023, https://bylinetimes.com/2023/09/22/editorial-the-populist-brand/

87 Dan Evans and Tom Latchem, 'Dan Wootton reveals "regrets" and claims "dark forces" attacking GB News in response to Byline Times three-year investigation', *Byline Times*, 19 July 2023, https://bylinetimes.com/2023/07/19/dan-wootton-reveals-regrets-and-claims-dark-forces-attacking-gb-news-in-response-to-byline-times-three-year-investigation/

88 See Russell Brand channel, https://www.youtube.com/@RussellBrand

89 BBC Sunday Politics, 'Andrew Neil ridicules American conspiracy theorist on Sunday Politics video', *Guardian*, 9 June 2013, https://www.theguardian.com/media/video/2013/jun/09/andrew-neil-american-conspiracy-theorist-sunday-politics-video

90 Russell Brand spews total nonsense to his audience: https://www.youtube.com/watch?v=2-PDyhX3b3A

91 'How conspiracy theorists jumped to defend Russell Brand before allegations were even made', Independent, 20 September 2023, https://www.independent.co.uk/news/uk/crime/conspiracy-theories-russell-brand-elon-musk-andrew-tate-b2414800.html

92 ' Ed Miliband interviewed by Russell Brand: the highlights', *Guardian*, 29 April 2015, https://www.theguardian.com/politics/video/2015/apr/29/ed-miliband-russell-brand-video-highlights

93 'Russell Brand's Revolution: Interview with Owen Jones', Guardian Live, 8 December 2014, https://www.youtube.com/watch?v=JduqBw2jIbo&ab_channel=GuardianLive

94 George Monbiot, 'I once admired Russell Brand, but his grim trajectory shows us where politics is heading', *Guardian*, 10 March 2023, https://www.theguardian.com/commentisfree/2023/mar/10/russell-brand-politics-public-figures-responsibility

95 Peter Guest, 'The Dark Economics of Russell Brand', *Wired*, 18 September 2023, https://www.wired.com/story/dark-economics-russell-brand/

96 Brian Stelter, 'The infamous Steve Bannon quote is key to understanding America's crazy politics', CNN, 16 November 2021, https://edition.cnn.com/2021/11/16/media/steve-bannon-reliable-sources/index.html

97 'Trump's LANDSLIDE Iowa Win – MSNBC FREAKOUT', Rumble, 16 January 2024, https://rumble.com/v47btc0-trumps-landslide-iowa-win-msnbc-freak-out-stay-free-285.html

98 The National Conservatism Conference was held 15–17 May 2023, The Emmanuel Centre, 9–23 Marsham St, London SW1P 3DW.

99 Intelligence Squared is the biggest London based organisation of its kind which puts on debates and panel discussions with big names in live venues.

100 He is president of the Herzl Institute in Jerusalem and serves as the chairman of the Edmund Burke Foundation. He has argued for national conservatism in his 2018 book *The Virtue of Nationalism* and 2022's *Conservatism: A Rediscovery*.

101 Peter Geoghegan, 'At NatCon London', *London Review of Books*, 1 June 2023, https://www.lrb.co.uk/the-paper/v45/n11/peter-geoghegan/short-cuts

102 Viktor Orbán is a Hungarian lawyer and politician who has been prime minister of Hungary since 2010.

103 Emeritus Professor of Sociology at the University of Kent.

104 Tortoise Media is a multiplatform media organisation set up by James Harding, former editor of the *Times*, and after that head of BBC News.

105 Michael Crick, *One Party After Another: The Disruptive Life of Nigel Farage*, Simon & Schuster, 2022.

106 Co-founder with Danny Kruger of the New Social Convenent Unit, established in 2021.

107 Speech made at National Conservatism Conference, London, 15 May 2023, https://www.youtube.com/watch?v=Bx3ei0Q2d6Y

108 Will Loyd, 'Miriam Cates: The Radical Traditionalist', *New Statesman*, 7 February 2024, https://www.newstatesman.com/politics/politics-interview/2024/02/miriam-cates-radical-traditionalist-interview

109 Will Loyd, Danny Kruger, 'The Moral Condition of England is Worse', *New Statesman*, 30 August 2023, https://www.newstatesman.com/encounter/2023/08/danny-kruger-interview-tories-disunited-britain

110 Suella Braverman, speech to Conservative Party Conference, 4 October 2022, www.mark-jenkinson.co.uk/news/suella-braverman-2022-speech-conservative-party-conference

111 George Orwell, 'Notes on Nationalism', *Polemic*, May 1945.

112 Tice had been a long time donor and member of the Conservative Party until 2019, when he helped found Reform UK as chairman and later leader.

113 Reform Party UK Ltd – see Companies House entry 11694875.

114 https://www.theguardian.com/world/2024/apr/16/belgian-mayor-natcon-conference-braverman-farage-brussel

115 Lewis Baston, 'Lib Dem byelection win was spectacular, but Labour's may hurt Tories most', *The Guardian*, 24 June 2022, https://www.theguardian.com/politics/2022/jun/24/lib-dem-byelection-win-spectacular-labour-hurt-tories-most

116 Jennie King, 'Deny, Deceive, Delay Vol 2: Exposing New Trends in Climate Mis-and Disinformation at COP27', ISD Global, 19 January 2023, https://www.isdglobal.org/isd-publications/deny-deceive-delay-vol-2-exposing-new-trends-in-climate-mis-and-disinformation-at-cop27/

117 The phrase 'energy independence' was the most common (1925 ads) in Meta's Ad Library, followed by 'American energy' (1558 ads). ISD Global, https://www.isdglobal.org › uploads › 2023/01

118 Brendan O'Neill, *Mail Online*, 26 September 2023 https://www.dailymail.co.uk/debate/article-12559631/BRENDAN-ONEILL-Rishi-Sunak-culture-warriors-eco-zealots-sex-offenders.html

119 Brendan O'Neill, *Spiked*, 21 March 2023, https://www.spiked-online.com/2023/03/21/eco-dread-is-a-luxury-belief-we-can-no-longer-afford/

120 'Bill Gates' "microchip" conspiracy theory and other vaccine claims fact-checked', BBC News, 30 May 2020, https://www.bbc.co.uk/news/52847648

121 Jabed Ahmed, 'One Month after Ulez Expanded, Uxbridge Residents are Still Angry', *Independent*, 1 October 2023.

122 Esther Addley, 'Study shows 60% of Britons believe in conspiracy theories', *Guardian*, 23 November 2018, https://www.theguardian.com/society/2018/nov/23/study-shows-60-of-britons-believe-in-conspiracy-theories

123 The Great Replacement conspiracy theory is a white supremacist, xenophobic, and anti-immigrant concept that posits white people are being replaced by immigrants, Muslims and other people of colour in their so-called 'home' countries. The conspiracy often blames the 'elite' and Jews for orchestrating these changing demographics. The Great Replacement was conceived of by a Frenchman, Renaud Camus, who popularised the idea in his 2011 book *Le Grand Remplacement.*

124 'The World's Real Time Billionaires 2024', *Forbes*, https://www.forbes.com/real-time-billionaires/#2397594d3d78

125 Mattias Ekman, 'The Great Replacement: Strategic mainstreaming of far-right conspiracy claims', *Sage Journal*, 6 May 2022, https://journals.sagepub.com/doi/full/10.1177/13548565221091983

126 Statista Research Department, 'Islam in the UK Statistics and Facts', 20 December 2023, https://www.statista.com/topics/4765/islam-in-the-united-kingdom-uk/#topicOverview

127 Olafimihan Oshin, '6 in 10 Trump voters agree with core tenet of Great Replacement Theory Survey', *The Hill*, 24 May 2022, *https://thehill.com/homenews/state-watch/3499877-6-in-10-trump-voters-agree-with-core-tenet-of-great-replacement-theory-survey/*

128   Anna Soubry, Twitter/X, 24 February 2024, https://twitter.com/Anna_Soubry/status/1761423543970013535

129   Media Reform, 'Who Owns the Media 2023' report, https://www.mediareform.org.uk/resources/reports

130 Press coverage of the refugee and migrant crisis in the EU.

131   Pew Research Center, 'A Wider Ideological Gap Between More and Less Educated Adults', 26 April 2016, https://www.pewresearch.org/politics/2016/04/26/a-wider-ideological-gap-between-more-and-less-educated-adults/

132 Jennifer C Kerr, 'Trump overwhelmingly leads rivals in support from less educated Americans', PBS News, 3 April 2016, https://www.pbs.org/newshour/politics/trump-overwhelmingly-leads-rivals-in-support-from-less-educated-americans

133 Melissa Fares *and* Gina Cherelus, 'Trump loves "the poorly educated" … and social media clamors', Reuters, 24 February 2016, https://www.reuters.com/article/idUSKCN0VX2DE/

134 Zack Stanton, 'How the Culture War could break democracy', Politico, 20 May 2021, https://www.politico.com/news/magazine/2021/05/20/culture-war-politics-2021-democracy-analysis-489900

135   Angie Drobnic Holan, 'In Context: Donald Trumps Very Fine People on Both Sides Remarks', *Politifact*, 26 April 2019, https://www.politifact.com/article/2019/apr/26/context-trumps-very-fine-people-both-sides-remarks/

136 Peter Walker, 'Heavy election defeat could lead to Tory Party lurch to right, analysis shows', *Guardian*, 28 December 2023, https://www.theguardian.com/politics/2023/dec/28/heavy-election-defeat-could-lead-to-tory-lurch-to-right-analysis-shows

137 Benedict Brogan, Boris Johnson interview: 'My advice to David Cameron? I've made savings, so can you', *Telegraph*, 29 April 2010, https://www.telegraph.co.uk/news/election-2010/7653636/Boris-Johnson-interview-My-advice-to-David-Cameron-Ive-made-savings-so-can-you.html

138 'Boris Johnson: Another Trump presidency could be "good for the world and America"', *Daily Mail*, 19 January 2024, https://www.dailymail.co.uk/video/borisjohnson/video-3104813/Video-Boris-Johnson-Trump-presidency-good-America.html

139 S. G. Tallentyre, 'Helvétius: The Contradiction', *The Friends of Voltaire*. Smith, Elder, & Co. p. 199, 1906, via Internet Archive.

140 1848 mood is the 'spirit of revolution across Europe'. There were a lot of rumours of revolutions across Europe which didn't quite come to pass.

141 Conservative Party Conference, Winter Gardens, Blackpool, 10 October 1975.

142 Let us Face the Future 1945: Manifesto, https://www.chartist.org.uk/let-us-face-the-future-1945/

143 Malcolm Dean, Obituary: Lord Young of Dartington, *Guardian*, 16 January 2002, https://www.theguardian.com/news/2002/jan/16/guardianobituaries.books

144   Tim Fountain and Toby Young, https://www.timfountain.co.uk/Tim_Fountain/How_To_Lose_Friends.html

145   Ronald Brownstein, 'The Book Bans Debate Has Finally Reached a Turning Point', 10 May 2023, *The Atlantic*, https://www.theatlantic.com/politics/archive/2023/05/gop-book-bans-democrats-state-legislation/674003/

146   Free Speech Union homepage, https://freespeechunion.org/

147   About the FSU, https://freespeechunion.org/about/

148   Freddie Attenborough, 'An £800,000 lesson in How Not to do Diversity Training', *The Critic*, 8 January 2024, https://thecritic.co.uk/an-800000-lesson-in-how-not-to-do-diversity-training/

149   Freddie Attenborough, "One of the Most Sinister Things I've Seen': Helen Joyce Reacts to Case of FSU Member Linzi Smith', *Free Speech Union*, 4 February 2024,   https://freespeechunion.org/one-of-the-most-sinister-things-ive-seen-helen-joyce-reacts-to-case-of-fsu-member-linzi-smith/

150   Gordon Rayner, 'Football fan banned gender critical posts after 'Stasi' Premier League', *Telegraph*, 2 February 2024, https://www.telegraph.co.uk/news/2024/02/02/football-fan-banned-gender-critical-posts-permier-league/

151   Linzi Smith and Julie Bindel (Canny Campaigners), 'The Word is Women', 5 February 2024, https://www.youtube.com/watch?v=daNVoKgrd3k

152   Linzi Smith, 'Banned and Spied on for my Beliefs', *Crowd Justice*, https://www.crowdjustice.com/case/linzi-smith-banned-spied-on/

153   Free Speech Union, 'FSU Party Vox Pop', 13 March 2024, https://youtu.be/X-9bg7f9rOk?t=631 (10:33 minute mark)

154   DeSmog, 'The Institute of Public Affairs', https://www.desmog.com/institute-public-affairs/

155   Tory Shepherd, 'A trade union for free speech? Battle lines drawn over groups that claim representative status', *Guardian*, 7 March 2024, https://www.theguardian.com/australia-news/2024/mar/08/free-speech-union-australia-members-fees-tax-deduction-unregistered-actu

156   Suzanne Moore, 'I'd never heard of Laurence Fox until he started lecturing us about racism', *Guardian*, 20 January 2020, https://www.theguardian.com/uk-news/commentisfree/2020/jan/20/id-never-heard-of-laurence-fox-until-he-started-lecturing-us-about-racism

157   Jamie Doward, *Observer*, 18 January 2020, https://www.theguardian.com/tv-and-radio/2020/jan/18/question-time-clash-lecturer-tells-of-hate-mail

158   Bethany Dawson, *Independent*, 9 May 2021, https://www.independent.co.uk/news/uk/politics/laurence-fox-london-mayor-lose-deposit-b1844481.html

159   In a 2015 essay for the Australian publication *The Quadrant*, entitled 'The fall of the meritocracy', under a section headed 'Progressive eugenics', Young proposed that poorer people should be helped to choose which embryos were allowed to develop, based on intelligence, *Guardian*, January 2018.

160   Nafeez Ahmed, 'For Whom the Bell Curves: Advisory to Johnson's Levelling Up Ally Hosts Race Science Extremist', Byline Times, 26 November 2021, https://bylinetimes.com/2021/11/26/for-whom-the-bell-curves-advisor-to-johnsons-levelling-up-ally-hosts-race-science-extremist/

161   Founded in 2015 by journalist Claire Lehmann, Quilette is an online Australia-based magazine that focuses on science, technology, news, culture and politics.

162   Robin de Peyer, 'Toby Young Tweets: The comments that led to his resignation', *Evening Standard*, January 2018, https://www.standard.co.uk/news/uk/toby-young-tweets-the-controversial-comments-that-led-to-his-resignation-a3735326.html

163   Nafeez Ahmed, 'Peter Theil's Free Speech for Race Science Crusade at Cambridge University Revealed', *Byline Times*, 10 December 2021, https://bylinetimes.com/2021/12/10/peter-thiels-free-speech-for-race-science-crusade-at-cambridge-university-revealed/

164   Toby Young, 'A Dispatch from the Woke Wars', NatCon UK, YouTube, 2023, https://www.youtube.com/watch?v=8vFN6LWBAeM&ab_channel=NationalConservatism

165   See Chapter 9 explaining the Great Replacement theory.

166   Gian Volpicelli, 'From Trotsky to Brexit to Orbán's attack dog: The man leading Hungary's fightback against the EU', Politico, 9 May 2023.

167   https://www.battleofideas.org.uk/session/revitalising-free-speech-on-campus-living-freedom-and-speak-easy/

168   https://bylinetimes.com/2022/06/08/charity-linked-to-viktor-Orbán-wants-to-take-over-british-schools-to-promote-far-right-pro-russia-propaganda/

169   Oliver O'Connell, 'Capitol Rioter who "hit cops with fire extinguisher" bused to DC by Turning Points USA', *Independent*, 3 March 2021, https://www.independent.co.uk/news/world/americas/capitol-riot-fire-extinguisher-charlie-kirk-bus-b1812096.html

170   Archie Bland, 'Students quit free speech campaign over role of Toby Young-founded group', *Guardian*, 9 January 2021, https://www.theguardian.com/media/2021/jan/09/students-quit-free-speech-campaign-over-role-of-toby-young-founded-group

171   Polly Toynbee, 'Paul Dacre, Daily Mail poisoner-in-chief is quitting. Good riddance', *Guardian*, 7 June 2018, https://www.theguardian.com/commentisfree/2018/jun/07/paul-dacre-gone-daily-mail-next-associated-newspapers

172   Oxfam, 'Richest 1% grab nearly twice as much new wealth as the rest of the world put together', 16 January 2023, https://www.oxfam.org.uk/media/press-releases/richest-1-grab-nearly-twice-as-much-new-wealth-as-rest-of-the-world-put-together/

173   Savage, M., Devine, F., Cunningham, N., et al, 'A New Model of Social Class? Findings from the BBC's Great British Class Survey Experiment', *Sociology* 47(2).

174   Media Reform 2023 Report: *Who Owns the UK Media?* https://www.mediareform.org.uk/wp-content/uploads/2023/10/Who-Owns-the-UK-Media-2023.pdf

175   Also the current employers of Zewditu Gebreyohanes, former head of Restore Trust – see Chapter 5.

176   Paul Sandle, 'Rupert Murdoch hires Piers Morgan in global TV, newspaper and book deal', *Reuters*, 16 September 2021, https://www.reuters.com/business/media-telecom/uks-piers-morgan-joins-rupert-murdochs-fox-news-global-deal-2021-09-16/

177   Ewan Somerville, 'Pupil who questioned classmate "identifying as a cat"

called "despicable" by teacher'. *Telegraph*, 18 June 2023, https://www.telegraph.co.uk/news/2023/06/18/pupil-teacher-despicable-identifying-cat-transgender/#

178   Nesrine Malik, 'It doesn't matter if a girl identified as a cat (she didn't). The issue is how post-truth politics exploits it', *Guardian*, 26 June 2023, https://www.telegraph.co.uk/news/2023/06/18/pupil-teacher-despicable-identifying-cat-transgender/#:

179   Tom Pyman, 'The rise of the "furries": How schools are allowing kids to identify as cats, horses and dinosaurs – and teachers are 'failing to question them', *Daily Mail*, 20 June 2023.

180   Arthur Parashar, 'Headteachers should intervene to stop children identifying as cats, horses, moons or other "neo" genders Downing Street says', *Daily Mail*, 20 June 2023, https://www.dailymail.co.uk/news/article-12215867/Headteachers-intervene-stop-children-identifying-cats-Downing-Street-says.html

181   Richard Adams, "Child identifying as cat controversy: from TikTok video to media frenzy', *Guardian*, 23 June 2023, https://www.theguardian.com/education/2023/jun/23/child-identifying-as-cat-controversy-from-a-tiktok-video-to-media-frenzy

182   Louisa Clarence-Smith, 'Kemi Badenoch calls for snap inspection of school in "cat gender" row', *Telegraph*,
23 June 2023, https://www.telegraph.co.uk/news/2023/06/23/kemi-badenoch-rye-college-cat-gender-inspection-ofsted/

183   Amy Walker, 'Trans people twice as likely to be victims of crime in England and Wales', *Guardian*, 17 July 2020, https://www.theguardian.com/society/2020/jul/17/trans-people-twice-as-likely-to-be-victims-of-in-england-and-wales

184   'Megyn Kelly blasts ESPN for honouring transgender swimmer Lia Thomas as part of Women's History Month Celebration', *Daily Mail*, 27 March 2023, https://www.dailymail.co.uk/news/article-11908513/Oh-hell-no-Megyn-Kelly-blasts-ESPN-honoring-transgender-swimmer-Lia-Thomas.html

185   Helen Joyce, *Trans: When Ideology Meets Reality*, Oneworld publications, 2021. Ms Joyce was educated at Trinity College Dublin; she has a MASt at the University of Cambridge and a PhD at University College London.

186   Jane Clare Jones, '"Someone has to be the Someone": An Interview with Helen Joyce', *The Radical Notion* Issue 4, https://theradicalnotion.org/someone-has-to-be-the-someone-an-interview-with-helen-joyce/

187   National Library of Medicine, https://pubmed.ncbi.nlm.nih.gov/37556147

188   Caroline Lowbridge, 'The lesbians who feel pressured to have sex and relationships with trans women', *BBC News*, 26 October 2021, https://www.bbc.co.uk/news/uk-england-57853385

189   Talk TV, 'Julia Hartley-Brewer in Conversation with Kathleen Stock', June 2023, https://www.youtube.com/watch?v=Gp8GtDNtCj4

190   Julie Bindel, 'Stock: I won't be silenced', *UnHerd*, 4 November 2021, https://unherd.com/2021/11/kathleen-stock-i-wont-be-silenced/

191   Kathleen Stock, 'I came out late – only to find that lesbians had slipped to the back of the queue', *Guardian*, 12 March 2023, https://www.theguardian.com/commentisfree/2023/mar/12/i-came-out-late-only-to-findlesbians-slipped-back-of-queu

192 Mermaids vs 1. Charity Commission for England & Wales 2. LGB Alliance Report, 9–16 September 2022, 7–8 November 2022, decision given on 6 July 2023.

193 Max Colbert, 'Tufton Street-Linked Trans-Exclusionary Charity Receives Surge in Funding', *Byline Times*, 21 August 2023, https://bylinetimes.com/2023/08/21/tufton-street-linked-trans-exclusionary-charity-receives-surge-in-funding/

194 Michael Cowan and Hollie Cole, 'Transgender Patients could face Years-Long Wait For NHS Treatment', BBC News, 20 March 2024, https://www.bbc.co.uk/news/uk-68602939

195 The Cass Review, https://cass.independent-review.uk/home/publications/final-report/

196 Peter Tatchell, 'Support both trans and women's liberation', 29 November 2021, https://www.petertatchellfoundation.org/support-both-trans-and-womens-liberation/

197 Peter Tatchell, 'UK Equality Minister says NO to meeting LGBT+ groups', 28 February 2024, https://www.petertatchellfoundation.org/uk-equality-minister-says-no-to-meeting-lgbt-groups-2/

198 Kemi Badenoch's letter to Peter Tatchell, 26 February 24, https://www.petertatchellfoundation.org/wp-content/uploads/2024/02/MC2024_00718-Response-1.pdf

199 Consolidated Analysis Center, incorporated (founded in 1967) is a business consultancy which invented ACORN (Association of Community Organizations for Reform Now), https://www.caci.co.uk/

200 Dr Joel Rogers de Waal, ' Brexit and Trump voters are more likely to believe in conspiracy theories', YouGov, 14 December 2018. Statistics from CRASSH, the Centre for Research in the Arts, Humanities and Social Sciences, Cambridge.

201 Abigail Abrams, 'Here's What We Know So Far about Russia's 2016 Meddling', *Time*, 18 April 2019, https://time.com/5565991/russia-influence-2016-election/

202 Evan Garcia, 'Who Stormed the US Capitol New Report Digs into Demographics of those Arrested', *WTTW*, 7 April 7 2021, https://news.wttw.com/2021/04/07/who-stormed-us-capitol-new-report-digs-demographics-those-arrested

203 Giles Whittell, 'How Somerset Capital tanked', *Tortoise Media*, 8 December 2023, https://www.tortoisemedia.com/2023/12/08/how-somerset-capital-tanked/.

204 Think tanks... or lobbying organisations?

205 'Government Challenged Over Massive Hike to Election Spending Limit Which is Set to Benefit Conservatives', *Byline Times*, 30 November 2023, https://bylinetimes.com/2023/11/30/government-challenged-over-massive-hike-to-election-spending-limit-which-is-set-to-benefit-conservatives/

206 Peter Walker and Rowena Mason, 'Tories urged to return "further £5m donation made by Frank Hester"', *Guardian*, 14 March 2024, https://www.theguardian.com/business/2024/mar/14/tories-urged-return-further-5m-donation-frank-hester

207 John Stevens and Mikey Smith, 'First Ever Partygate video revealed as Tories drink, dance and laugh at Covid rules', *Mirror*, updated 19 June 2023, https://www.mirror.co.uk/news/politics/first-ever-partygate-video-revealed-30259486

208 Robert T McKenzie, *Angels in Marble: Working Class Conservatives in Urban England*, Heinemann Educational Publishers, 1968.

209 Dominic Penna, 'Tory campaign manager behind 2019 landslide to return amid early election speculation', *Telegraph*, 23 November 2023.

210 Boris Johnson, 'The global wokerati are trembling so violently you can hear the ice tinkling in their negronis... but a Trump presidency could be just what the world needs', *Daily Mail*, 19 January 2024.

211 Adam Forrest, 'Rishi Sunak suggests Nigel Farage welcome to re-join "broad church" Tories', *Independent*, 4 December 2023.

212 Matthew Jim Elliott, Baron Elliott of Mickle Fell, FRSA (born 12 February 1978) is a British political strategist and lobbyist who has served as the chief executive of a number of organisations and been involved in various referendum campaigns, including Vote Leave. Elliott was the founder and has served as chief executive of the TaxPayers' Alliance in 2004, Big Brother Watch and Business for Britain.

213 New Culture Forum, 'Our Aims', https://www.newcultureforum.org.uk/our-aims

214 Matt Honeycombe-Foster: 'London Influence: IEA way or The Highway', Politico, 8th September 2022

215 Atlas Network (formerly Atlas Economic Research Foundation) is a non-governmental 501c3 organisation based in the US. It provides training, networking and grant for libertarian, free-market and conservative groups around the world. Brad Lips has been the CEO of Atlas Network since 2009.

216 George Monbiot, 'Right-wing think tanks run this government, but first they had to capture the BBC', *Guardian*, 5 October 2022.

217 Nikolaus Pevsner, *Buildings of England London 6: Westminster*, pp. 89, 672, 708.

218 William Wallace, 'Follow the Money', Research Professional News, 4 December 2022, https://www.researchprofessionalnews.com/rr-news-uk-views-of-the-uk-2022-12-follow-the-money/

219 The Transparency of Lobbying, Non-Party Campaigning and Trade Union Administration Act.

220 Simon Yaffe, 'Strategist was Inquisitive about the World from Age of 11', *Jewish Telegraph*, 2016 https://www.jewishtelegraph.com/prof_369.html. My emphasis.

221 Alexandra Jaffe, 'Bobby Jindal slams "no go zones" pushes assimilation', CNN, 21 January 2015, https://edition.cnn.com/2015/01/19/politics/jindal-no-go-zones-london/index.html

222 Ned Simons, 'Bobby Jindal Talking "Complete Nonsense" says London Mayor Boris Johnson', *Huffington Post*, 13 February 2015.

223 Zoe Grunewald, 'Tory MP Paul Scully resigns after warning of "no-go" areas in London and Birmingham', Yahoo News, 4 March 2024.

224 Patel, Reyhana, 'NUS condemns "anti-Islam" group Student Rights', *Independent*, 14 May 2014.

225 Rishi Sunak's 1 March 2024 Address on Extremism: https://www.gov.uk/government/speeches/pm-address-on-extremism-1-march-2024

226 Vikram Dodd, 'Antisemitic hate crimes in London up 1350%, Met Police say', *Guardian*, 20 October 2023, https://www.theguardian.com/news/2023/oct/20/antisemitic-hate-crimes-in-london-rise-1350-since-israel-hamas-war-met-says

227 Nafeez Ahmed, 'Trumpocracy in the UK: Boris Johnson's Lobby Group US Dark Money', *Byline Times*, 3 November 2020, https://bylinetimes.com/2020/11/03/trumpocracy-in-the-uk-boris-johnsons-lobby-group-us-dark-money/

228 See Chapter 3: Matthew d'Ancona, 'Bannon's Britain', Tortoise Media, 28 September 2019.

229 Charles Hymas, 'Pro-Palestinian protests making London a "no-go zone" for Jews', *Telegraph*, 7 March 2024.

230 Matt Kennard, 'Priti Patal was part of CIA-linked lobby group with husband of Assange Judge', Declassified UK, 29 March 2022.

231 Andrew Gimson, 'Book Review: Murray tries and fails to stir up a panic about "a war on the west"', Conservative Home, 27 May 2022, https://conservativehome.com/2022/05/27/book-review-murray-tries-and-fails-to-stir-up-panic-about-the-war-on-the-west-by-anti-racist-campaigners/

232 Jasper Jolly, 'Daily Mail publisher to delist from stock market after 90 years', *Guardian*, 16 December 2021, https://www.theguardian.com/business/2021/dec/16/daily-mail-general-trust-publisher-delist-stock-market-lord-rothermere-dmgt

233 Joe Mellor, 'Mail asks Sunak to explain tax arrangements', The London Economic, 4 November 2022, https://www.thelondoneconomic.com/news/mail-asks-sunak-to-explain-tax-arrangements-ignoring-that-their-owner-is-a-non-dom-himself-319029/

234 James Bartholomew, 'I invented virtue signalling, now it's taking over the world', *Spectator*, 10 October 2015, https://www.spectator.co.uk/article/i-invented-virtue-signalling-now-it-s-taking-over-the-world/

235 Will Englund, 'Why Trump's "enemy of the people" bluster can't be compared to Stalin's savage rule', *Washington Post*, 17 January 2018, https://www.washingtonpost.com/news/retropolis/wp/2018/01/16/why-trumps-enemy-of-the-people-bluster-cant-be-compared-to-stalins-rule/

236 Rowena Mason, 'Dominic Cummings think-tank called for "end of BBC in current form"', *Guardian*, 21 January 2020, https://www.theguardian.com/politics/2020/jan/21/dominic-cummings-thinktank-called-for-end-of-bbc-in-current-form

237 Tom Harper and Oliver Shah, 'Christopher Chandler: Russian Spy? Money man for Putin and Trump? "No I'm just a shy billionaire"', *Times*, 13 May 2018, https://www.thetimes.co.uk/article/christopher-chandler-spy-money-man-for-putin-and-trump-no-im-just-a-shy-billionaire-2h58mbmqh

238 Tom Standen-Jewell, Arthur Fooks and Gill Hind, 'TalkTV and GB News', Enders Analysis Report, p. 3, 4 July 2023.

239 Jake Kanter, 'GB News was the biggest mistake in my career, says Andrew

Neil', *Times*, 17 November 2021, https://www.thetimes.co.uk/article/gb-news-was-biggest-mistake-of-my-career-says-andrew-neil-j9lx7nwnx

240 Update on GB News Impartiality Cases: Ofcom Report, 23 October 2023.

241 Dan Evans and Tom Latchem, 'GB News Star Dan Wootton Unmasked in Cash-for-sexual-images Catfishing Scandal', *Byline Times*, 17 July 2023 https://bylinetimes.com/2023/07/17/gb-news-star-dan-wootton-unmasked-in-cash-for-sexual-images-catfishing-scandal/

242 Christopher Williams, 'GB News owner in talks with US billionaire over Telegraph bid', *Telegraph*, 25 September 2023, https://www.telegraph.co.uk/business/2023/09/25/telegraph-sale-gb-news-owner-talks-ken-griffin/

243 Andrew Neil, 'With Britain turning Left just as the rest of Europe turns right, I fear that as PM, Keir Starmer would find his honey rather short', *Daily Mail*, 16 March 2024.

244 See note 210.

245 Zack Stanton, 'How Culture Wars could break Democracy', Politico, 20 May 2021, https://www.politico.com/news/magazine/2021/05/20/culture-war-politics-2021-democracy-analysis-489900

About the author and illustrator

Peter York is an author/journalist/broadcaster and a management consultant – a capitalist tool. Under both hats, the subject of social groupings and market segments is his major preoccupation. His earliest and best-known description of a social group came in his bestselling book *The Official Sloane Ranger Handbook*, which he co-authored with Ann Barr. Since then, he has charted the fortunes of many elite groupings, from designers ('chic-graphique') to television types to the Westminster illiberal elite. He believes that while sociologists and market researchers are forever studying The Rest of Us, the people at the top have escaped scrutiny for too long.

Peter started writing as style editor at *Harper's & Queen* and over the last 40 years he has produced a flood of broadsheet articles and 12 books (including this one). He has also contributed to television programmes from *The Tube* to *Newsnight* and made some of his own, including two series, one on style and one on the 1980s, and a number of single authored documentaries, including *The Rise and Fall of the Adman*, all for BBC2 and *Peter York's Hipster Handbook* for BBC4.

Peter is a former president of the Media Society. He is also a visiting professor at the University of the Arts London, a former board trustee of the Prince of Wales' Charity Arts & Business and of the Tate Members' Council. He recently set up the Pimlico Society with author Clive Aslet to help the oppressed people of Pimlico in their struggle for self-determination. He writes a monthly column for *Byline Times* about the metropolitan illiberal elite.

Martin Rowson is a multi-award-winning cartoonist, illustrator, author, performer, broadcaster and poet. Over the past four decades his work has appeared in almost every publication you can think of, from the *Guardian* to the *Erotic Review*, from the *Spectator* to the *Morning Star*, via the *Times, Tribune, Daily Mirror, New Statesman, Irish Times, Independent on Sunday, Time Out, Racing Post* and even, once, the *Daily Mail*. In fact, about the only places he hasn't appeared are the *Sun* (they've never asked) and *Private Eye* (don't ask). *Byline Times* is one of his current haunts.

He's also authored more than 40 books, including graphic novelisations of *The Waste Land, Gulliver's Travels, The Life and Opinions of Tristram Shandy, Gentleman* and *The Communist Manifesto*. He has illustrated books by Will Self, John Sweeney, Philippe Sands and many others, while *Stuff*, his 2006 memoir about clearing out his late parents' house, was longlisted for the Samuel Johnson Prize. His seven volumes of poetry will be augmented in December 2024 by his updated rewriting of Alexander Pope's *The Dunciad*.

Between 2000 and 2008 Rowson served as Ken Livingstone's Cartoonist Laureate for London (a post subsequently abolished by Boris Johnson). He has served for over 30 years as a trustee of the Zoological Society of London, which awarded him with an honorary fellowship, its highest honour, in 2023 and is also an honorary fellow of Goldsmith's College and has an honorary doctorate awarded by the University of Westminster.

Examples of his work are held in the collections of the National Portrait Gallery, the British Museum and the Museum of London, as well as the downstairs toilet galleries of politicians of all stripes. Each year he also daubs on walls at festivals from south-east London to south-west Wales, and regularly performs his ever-changing one-man stage show around the UK and beyond.

Rowson lives in Lewisham with his wife, visited now and again by their adult children when they're passing. In 2018, in a full page editorial responding to one of his *Guardian* cartoons, the *Daily Mail* described him and his work as "Disgusting... deranged... sick and offensive", which he counts as the greatest compliment ever paid him.